BECAUSE I SAID SO

A guide to negotiating with children and grown ups

Barry J. Elms

ISBN: 061559221X
ISBN-13: 978-0615592213

Contents

Foreword

Thank you for checking out my book. I should point out before you read any further, that I am not a child psychologist and that this is not a how to book for improving parenting skills. I am a business coach and also a parent and my goal is to demonstrate how the negotiating skills that have served me well in the business arena are the same skills that I used to resolve issues with my children.

The book is laced with stories of my business and personal exploits giving the reader an insight into the mind of a professional negotiator. Many of the stories give a detailed blow by blow account of problems that I have resolved in business and in my family life showing the direct parallel between both business and personal negotiating skills.

Because I have chosen to relate real examples from my family life as well as my corporate experiences this book contains stories that are very personal in nature which I hope adds to the authenticity of my messages. Where appropriate I have used humor to lighten the mood and entertain the reader. Most importantly this book is my attempt to give you, the reader, a legitimate game plan for negotiating practical solutions to all of life's day to day challenges, whether they are with business associates, friends or family members.

One word of caution, don't let your children read this book unless you want them to be as good a negotiator as you are.

PART ONE

Controlling the Elements

"The outcome of all negotiations is controlled by 5 elements. The ability to be an effective negotiator and secure successful deals depends on how well you use these elements to your advantage."

- From my seminar THE COMPLETE NEGOTIATOR

Chapter 1

THE GAME PLAN

I f you have children or were at one time a small child you are familiar with the classic parental power play *because I said so.* How wonderful it was when your children actually did what you asked simply because you said so. If only that could last forever and work every time on everyone.

Well, it's not going to happen. But don't despair, all is not lost, you can still get agreement without resentment if you understand how the process of negotiating works. And you better figure it out because your kids have and they are experts at playing you, or at least driving you crazy and frustrating your efforts to get cooperation.

As a professional negotiator I have discovered a wonderful secret formula for getting what you want from children and adults alike. It's not going to be a secret for much longer, however, because I am going to share it with you. Here's what I know:

EVERYTHING THAT HAPPENS IN YOUR INTERACTIONS WITH OTHERS IS ONE OR MORE OF 5 ELEMENTS IN ACTION. CONTROL THE 5 ELEMENTS AND YOU WILL CONTROL THE OUTCOME.

Look at the 5 words I have listed below, because they are your passport to getting agreement in every interaction.

LOGIC
POWER
EMOTION
TRADE
COMPROMISE

Now, don't get excited because at this point they are just 5 words and until you know how they control everything they won't help you get anything. But can it really be true? Is it really as simple as doing 5 things well and you get agreement? Yes and yes!

I remember reading a book about Bill Belichick, the head coach for the New England Patriots, one of the most successful football coaches of all time. In the book the author was marveling at how Belichick prepared for each game. How he would spend all week, often for 12 hours or more each day, figuring out how to beat the opposing team. According to the book, at the end of the week of preparation he would gather his team together and explain to them that if they did 4 or 5 specific things well they would win the game. It would not necessarily be the same 4 or 5 things each week; they were bound to vary depending on the team they were trying to beat. But the point is legitimate, by distilling a full week of planning into a simple formula his team knew exactly what they needed to do to achieve success and, as results proved, when they followed the game plan to perfection they won the game.

My negotiating formula works on the same principle, if you follow my game plan and do 5 things well you will control the outcome of every interaction and get agreement every time. Sound too good to be true? Well let me prove it to you.

Let's start with a simple explanation of what each of the 5 elements represents in negotiations. When I have done that we can get to the fun part where I will show you how they work in real life negotiations, both with children and adults alike.

I am going to divide the 5 elements into 2 categories, primary and secondary. Under the heading of primary negotiating elements we have:

LOGIC
Logic is: the facts or merits of your case. Your ability to present an argument based on verifiable information or established facts.

POWER
Power is: The ability to penalize or reward. In effect it is your ability to describe the benefits or consequences to the other party.

EMOTION
Emotion is: the human element. The ability to connect with the other party's feelings.

These primary elements are a manifestation of life's persuasive skills. All people, children and adults alike, are persuaded to a point of view based on your ability to formulate an argument that includes all 3 elements. In simple terms, if you can convince the other party that you are right, and also that it is in their best interest to accept your position while at the same time show that you are being fair and reasonable, you will get what you want.

However, this is not a magic wand. If the other party thinks you are wrong, and also believes that you have no impact on them whatsoever and does not like you, you will get nothing.

Real life operates between those two extremes, which is why we need to understand the value of the secondary negotiating elements. Simply put, if Logic, Power and Emotion are your persuasive tools then the secondary elements of Trade and Compromise are your creative tools.

Here is a brief explanation of the secondary or creative negotiating elements:

TRADE
Trade is: something for something. It represents your ability to offer a fair exchange of value.

COMPROMISE
Compromise is: mutual or individual concession. Where one or both parties move from their original position in order to reach agreement.

Primary
LOGIC
POWER
EMOTION

Secondary
TRADE
COMPROMISE

Later in the book, as my story unfolds, I will share with you a separate formula for creating equal value trades, as well as a full understanding of how and when to use compromise to seal the deal. But, let me say that one of the most common mistakes people make when negotiating is to rush to compromise as a means to solve a problem. This is especially true with parents who are in a hurry to solve problems and move on. It is also true in the business world where deals are won and lost, so let me make one thing clear, do not make compromise your first thought in problem solving, as doing so often leads to unsatisfying solutions.

A story comes to my mind that I think proves my point that compromise should not be your first option.

This story relates to a speaking engagement I had with a group of attorneys at a conference in Chicago. I remember it this way. As I walked into the hotel ballroom to commence my presentation I saw that the room was jam packed with people. All six hundred seats were taken and there were people standing up lining the walls. The place was electric with chatter, creating an exciting atmosphere for my presentation. I went up on the stage area and began my opening remarks when something very interesting happened.

As I stood there warming up the crowd with microphone in hand a guy entered the room and started to march down the center aisle. I was thinking to myself, 'where are you going', not only were there no seats, there were clearly no seats, but this guy was not looking at seats he was looking at me and walking purposefully towards me on stage. All the time he was doing so I was thinking 'go right, go left, just go'. But he kept on coming and stepped up onto my stage. At that point the whole room went completely quiet, an amazing sight in and of itself if you can picture it, six hundred plus attorneys silent in anticipation of what might happen next.

As the guy walked across the stage toward me I stopped talking waiting for whatever was coming next. As the guy approached me he spoke clearly to me and, with the aid of my microphone, to the group in general. Here's what he said:

"We have a problem. We are having a meeting next door and we can't hear ourselves with your microphone so loud. We need you to turn it down".

My response was quick and simple, I said. "Who are you?" It seemed to me to make sense to start with that question because anyone who has the nerve to walk on stage and interrupt my session is likely to be either important or dangerous and I would like to know up front which of those options I am dealing with.

His reply did not help my cause. He said. "I am one of the senior executives of this group" pointing to the audience, "and we are having an executive meeting next door".

In the next moment, as I was thinking of an appropriate response, which included compromising by turning down my microphone just a little, something very interesting happened. The man who had invited me to speak at the event was sitting in the second row and looking very upset. He got out of his seat and marched up on the stage to join me and our executive interloper. He immediately took the executive aside and spoke urgently to him on the edge of the stage. I don't know what was said, but the guy from the other meeting left and never came back.

When I tell this story people often ask me why it was that the executive left so quickly. I don't know the answer to that because I was so grateful that he was no longer an intrusion that I did not follow up on that with my sponsor, I simply continued with my presentation. What I do know is that one of the following scenarios probably happened.

My sponsor may have said. "Look, John, you have twenty people at your meeting while I have six hundred attendees at this meeting. Don't you think it would make sense for you to contact the hotel management and have them find an alternative small meeting room for you where you would not be adversely affected by our noise?" – A position based on LOGIC.

Or he may have said. "You are disrupting this meeting, John, which over six hundred of our members have paid to listen to. If you value your executive status I suggest that you find an alternative room for your meeting." – A position based on POWER.

Alternatively he may have said something like. "Don't do this to me, John, I didn't want to have to manage this event in the first place and now you are risking making it a failure. Please help me out here and see if you can find another room for your meeting". – A position based on EMOTION.

Or maybe he was more creative and said something like this. "I tell what I can do, John, if you go to the hotel management and ask them to set you up in another small room for your meeting I will buy you dinner tonight, how about that?" - A position based on TRADE

As I said, I don't know which of those possible solutions worked, but what I do know is that the solution did not involve a COMPROMISE on my part as I continued my presentation as planned without lowering the volume on my microphone.

The message of this story is a simple one; just because *compromise* was my first thought it does not mean that it was my best option, as was clearly demonstrated by the final outcome.

Before considering a quick compromise solution in any interaction with children or adults firstly ask yourself if there is a better solution available based on any one or more of the other four negotiating elements.

As I have mentioned, later in the book I will spend time sharing my thoughts on how to come up with collaborative solutions based on the creative elements of *Trade* and *Compromise*. For now, I want to concentrate on how to use the three primary elements of *Logic, Power* and *Emotion* to be persuasive. The prevailing principle here is that good negotiators look for ways to support their position, not for ways to change it. I really believe that the best negotiators are not those who conjure up creative solutions, but those who present the most value for their point of view. To do that it is necessary to learn how to use and diffuse each of the primary elements to maximum effect.

As I have already stated, a combination of Logic, Power and Emotion represents the three legged stool of persuasion skills. The problem is that different people respond to different styles of persuasion. There is not one persuasive element that applies to all situations. For example:

For some people, if you demonstrate that the facts support your position they will recognize those facts and accept your point of view.

For other folks, you could give them the facts all day long, but until you demonstrate what's in it for them you will not get agreement.

For some other people, you can give them the facts and let them know what's in it for them, but if they don't like you or trust you, you are wasting your time.

The key to being persuasive is by understanding the thinking of the person you are trying to influence, and to use their mindset to your advantage. In any negotiation you would need to ask yourself; are they driven by *Logic, Power,* or *Emotion*? Whichever element they are focused on is the one you need to control.

If they are focused on *Logic,* then you need to have a logical argument to offset it.

If they are focused on *Power*, then you will need to address that power to resolve the problem.

If they are focused on *Emotion*, then you will need to deal with that emotion before you can find a solution to the issue at hand.

Before we can successfully get agreement from our children, or anyone else, we better understand which of the primary elements we are using and which ones are being used on us.

Now is a good time to put this formula to the test.

Chapter 2

PICK YOUR POISON

In order to demonstrate the value and impact of each primary negotiating position, I would like you to consider this question and make a choice:

What if, for the rest of your life, you could only have one persuasive element to use in negotiations, which one would you choose?

LOGIC, POWER or EMOTION

Remember, whichever one you choose, you will never be able to use the other two. I know it is an unfair question and that you would always want to have all three elements at your disposal, but humor me because it will help me demonstrate the value of each element.

However, before you decide, let me give you a sense of the ramifications of your choices. For example:

If you choose LOGIC you will always be right. No one will be able to argue with your facts. You will make it your modus operandi to always have the facts clearly identified. The problem will be that you will have no *power* over the other party and you will not be able to use *emotion* to develop likeability.

If you choose POWER you will develop a tough style of negotiating. You will be very comfortable telling others how it's going to be. You will have the classic "my way or the highway" personality. And you will be good at it. The problem will be that you have no facts to support your position and you will not be likeable.

If you choose EMOTION you will become likeable. You will be engaging in your interactions with others. People will like you and enjoy dealing with you. The problem is that you will have no power over anyone and you will have no facts to support your case.

I know these are stereotypes, but I have met people who meet each of those profiles.

So now you know the consequences of your choices. It's time to make a choice. Don't think it through, go with your instincts and pick one right now.

Okay, which one did you choose? LOGIC, POWER or EMOTION

I have asked this question of groups as small as 10 people and as large as 1000, at hundreds of seminars worldwide. Polling people from every walk of life, ethic background and job description and the answers almost always fall into the same categories.

The most popular answer is usually LOGIC, followed closely by EMOTION, with POWER almost always getting the least amount of votes.

Now, before you pat yourself on the back because you chose LOGIC or EMOTION, let me say this. Regardless of which choice you made, if you did not choose POWER, you probably fooled yourself. Okay, that is a bit harsh, but the fact is, I really believe that given a choice people would choose power, and I think I can prove it.

Let's go back to the parent child dynamic. How often do parents shut down any negotiations with their small children by using the power play of *because I said so*? All the time, right?

The question is why do parents use this obviously crude power play, unsupported by facts and with no likeability?

Answer: Because they can!

Thereby proving my point that given a choice people often gravitate toward POWER. I think the reason parents use the expression *because I said so* as a way to secure agreement is that when it works it works quickly, and quick solutions are very attractive in our busy lives.

The question then becomes; why does *because I said so* not last long as a means to get agreement?

Answer; because when it comes to using POWER as a solution to disagreement, the fact is, the more you use it the quicker you lose it. Power plays are subject to diminishing returns. There are only so many times that you can impose your will on others before they get tired of it and look for alternative solutions.

Most parents find that crude power plays have a relatively short life span, their children quickly become immune to *because I said so* and start to question the decisions of their parents, often by using the word *why* to try and refocus the discussion. I will explain more on how cleverly children can refocus a conversation later in the book, but for now I want to continue with my theme on how best to control the power position.

So, how long can a parent maintain an effective power play with a child? The answer, as I stated, depends partly on how often you use it, but also on how well you use it.

For example, most parents will admit that maintaining power over their children once they become teenagers is a constant struggle. Young teenagers are naturally rebellious, searching for ways to assert their independence and break the parental power grip. But don't despair, used effectively parents can maintain power over their teenagers without sacrificing a loving relationship. How is that possible, you may ask? Let me give you a demonstration, based on my own experience with one of my sons on the one occasion when he decided to test my power.

I am a big sports fan and the story relates to a period in my life when I owned a soccer team. It was one of those teams that high school boys or girls can join if they are looking to develop their skills to a high level and play in tournaments throughout the USA. We were originally part of a larger soccer club in Massachusetts but we had some conflict with the club and decided to be our own separate entity for 2 years. During that time my son was the captain of the team, no surprise there since I owned the team. However I was not the coach of the team and during our last year together the coach was looking for some preseason activity to prepare the boys for our full season ahead. He was able to secure our place in an indoor competition for six Saturday night games. This was not ideal because we play outdoors but it at least allowed the team to get some good practice in readiness for the season ahead.

One other problem was that there were eighteen boys on the team and it was a six aside competition and, like basketball, you can't have eighteen boys on the sidelines because too many of them would not get any playing time. The coach's solution was to have ten or twelve boys there each Saturday night and that the boys should work out a schedule whereby each of them played for 3 or 4 weeks of the 6 week competition. That worked for me, except that I wanted my son there every week because he was the captain of the team, and I would also be there each week as an example to my son. This worked fine for the first three weeks. It is on week four that this story really begins.

As chance would have it I was working on the Saturday in question speaking at a conference out of town. My flight back allowed me time to go to the game, but it was going to be tight. I alerted my son before I left to remember that we had a game on Saturday night and not to forget as I would not be around to remind him. "Yes dad" he said as I walked out the door.

If you have ever been on a plane you know there is always a chance for delays or cancellations and this day was one of those days. My flight home was delayed but I made it home just in time at around 6.00pm, which was cutting it tight because we had to leave at 6.30pm to make it to the game on time. As I walked in the house I saw my wife and asked her. "Is Scott ready to go to the game?" as I did not see him hanging around the house.
"He is not here" she replied.

Confused by her answer I asked her where he was. "He went to play pool with his buddy" she said.

Still confused I asked her how that was possible as he was supposed to be playing soccer that evening.

"His friend called him and he cleared it with the coach and off he went" she casually replied.

"Call him if you want" she continued. "He left about an hour ago".

My wife thought the whole episode was highly amusing as this was the first time our son had ever done anything like this. She had a phone in her hand and a smile on her face as she said again.
"Give him a call I want to see what happens".

The good thing is that these days all eighteen year olds have cell phones. The stupid thing is that he answered it. Strategically his best move would have been to ignore my call, working on the premise that it is better to ask for forgiveness than for permission. But he obviously thought he had a persuasive argument because he answered my call.

What may surprise you is how I began the conversation on the phone. I did not demand he return home or try to impose my will on him in any way. When he answered my call I simply asked this question in a very neutral tone. "Where are you, son?" That may seem like a strange opening question because I already know where he is, but hear me out. And it is not a gotcha question; I know that he is not going to lie about where he is, having told his mother where he was going and having cleared it with his coach.

As will be explained in detail in a later chapter I was, in fact, opening with a strategic move known in negotiations as *getting the agenda*. My goal at this early stage of the conversation was to establish his position in order to determine the most effective way to win the argument.

Here was his opening reply. "I'm playing pool dad. The fact is the coach does not need me as he has plenty of players. In fact it made sense for me not to go so that some of the other boys can have more playing time."

So there you have it. He was ready for my call and had an argument all prepared. If you took note of the 5 elements that I listed in the first chapter you will notice that my son was using *Logic* to support his decision to skip the soccer game.

I replied. "I understand the situation, son, but if you want to talk facts with me, the fact is you and I had an agreement to meet here and go to the game together. Have I got my facts right?"

By using facts as my response I was taking his logic based argument and neutralizing its impact with logic of my own. The premise being that if he really cared about the facts then he would recognize that my facts out weighed his. Simply put, my factual argument was that he had an agreement with me not with his coach and that he could not break the agreement with me simply because it was ok with someone else.

My goal was to use his fact based argument to my advantage and thereby get him to agree to my position. It didn't work.

What it did do, however, was force him to reconsider his position. He now realized that he no longer controlled the logical high ground. My facts effectively neutralized his. As soon as he realized this he did what anyone would do if they did not want to agree; he changed his argument.

His next move was to say: "I didn't think you would mind, dad. I never get to see my friends and I just needed a break. I have gone to the game every week and I thought you would be cool with it".

Nice move. Recognizing that facts were no longer his strong suit he moved to a position based on the element of *Emotion,* which is a popular second move in reaction to a failed logical play.

I was ready for that. Here was my reply: "I get it, son, I really do, and I know you just wanted to hang out. I don't have a problem with that. But if you want to talk about what's fair, you dumped me man, is that fair?"

What I did was move my argument to meet his. He wanted to now make it about what was fair, using an emotional appeal, so I simply used an emotional appeal of my own to neutralize his argument. It's like taking candy from a baby. I now paused to see if it worked. It didn't work.

But he is now out of gas. He had two positions in mind *Logic* and *Emotion* and he had used them both. Each time he did so I took his position and neutralized its value with arguments of my own. My *Logic* matched against his *Logic* and my *Emotion* matched against his *Emotion*.

Now what will he do? His two arguments based on *Logic* and *Emotion* did not work and I am convinced that he will not move to the third primary negotiating position: *Power*.

The reason I am convinced that I hold the power position has nothing to do with the fact that I am his father. Many teenagers are prepared to test the power of their parents. I hold the power position because I have two things he needs, and as long as I have those two things I control the power. What are the two things that give me the power? Keys and Cash, and as long as he believes I control those things he will not test my power.

So when his *Logic* and *Emotion* arguments failed him he had nothing left in the tank. In response to my neutralizing his emotional appeal he simply said: "Can I stay anyway?"

How lame is that? Don't get me wrong, if he had formulated a winning argument I would not have forced him to return home. It is never a good idea to make a power play against strong *Logic* and *Emotion* because it builds resentment. However, having neutralized both his logic and emotion positions I now am in a position to control the outcome. Here is what I said in response to "Can I stay anyway".

"Listen son. If you had called me we might have been able to work something out, but you didn't, and you don't break agreements, it is that simple. You should also know that we don't dump people in this family and you definitely don't get to dump me. Come home Scott you are going to the game, you do not want to be on the wrong side of me".

He was home in fifteen minutes. There was no long term resentment and we went to the game. My power play worked. Let's analyze why it worked.

Firstly, I did not start with a power play. My initial question to my son, 'where are you?' was designed to establish his position. Once I had his position I was then able to neutralize his arguments by using the same arguments, i.e. *logic* and then *emotion*.

Secondly, having neutralized his arguments I then summarized my case based on my own positions of *Logic* and *Emotion* before I integrated my power play.

In conclusion; by holding my power play until the end and only using my power when I had established that it was both right and fair to do so I was able to convince my son to do as I asked, without any lasting resentment. In fact he scored 3 goals and enjoyed the game. Afterwards I took him to dinner to congratulate him on his play and his decision making skills.

The important thing to remember about power is that it is better to have it than to use it and that you only have power if the other party thinks you do. Power perceived is power achieved.

To summarize the use of *Power* as a persuasive element:

When it works it usually works quickly.
When it does not work the result is often confrontation.
Power should not be used as an opening move; it works better as a closing position.
Power should be supported by *Logic* and *Emotion* so that it does not create resentment.
Power is subject to diminishing returns. The more you use it the quicker you lose it.

Later in the book I will share with you my approach to dealing with power plays that are directed at you by the person you are negotiating with. That is a whole different story. For now let's take a look at the consequences of selecting either *Emotion* or *Logic* as your only means of securing agreement.

Chapter 3

PEOPLE LIKE TO DO THINGS
FOR PEOPLE THEY LIKE

E arlier in the book I asked you to make a choice. I said:

If you could only use one of the three influencing factors, of *Logic, Power* or *Emotion*. Which one would you choose?

The second most popular choice at my seminars is usually *Emotion*. For many people the idea of using likeability to secure agreement is a very attractive option. Children in particular are very good at using emotional tactics when negotiating with parents. I think the reason children gravitate towards *Emotion* as a strategy to get agreement is that they instinctively know that *Emotion* is the best way to soften up the other party in a negotiation in order to draw them into a compromise solution. And who better to use an emotional appeal on than a loving parent.

Shortly I will share with you how I would handle an emotional appeal from a child, but firstly let me tell you a story about one of my adult clients who is very effective at using emotion to get agreement. This guy has tremendous likeability and he knows it. He just might be the best *Emotion* negotiator I have ever met.

The client in question is the president of a business association in Texas that I had worked with on several occasions and the story is about one time when he telephoned me at my office to soften me up over a deal he had in mind. Here's how the conversation unfolded.

Once we got past the 'hi' and 'how are you' opening stage of the call, he launched into his strategy this way.

"Barry" he said. "I have just been asked to manage the national convention for my association here in Texas next year and I want you to be my keynote speaker."

"Great" I replied. "It will be my pleasure".

At that point he made his move. "You know we love you down here man. You have presented several seminars for us over the years and my members think you are fantastic. But this is not a seminar, Barry, this is a huge conference and I have never done anything this big before and I don't even know if I can make a profit on the event. I want you to be the keynote guy but you are going to have to give me a break on your fees on this one".

So there we have it, the classic emotional appeal. He hit me with the 'help me out man' appeal and waited for my response.

This kind of emotional appeal is often very effective when used by someone you like or by someone you care about. It is designed to soften you up and to encourage responses such as:

"What do you need?" or "I will see what I can do".

Do not fall for it! The moment you reply with either of these responses you have been manipulated into a concession discussion which will cause you to move into the secondary negotiating stage of *Trade* or *Compromise*.

I am fully aware of the seductive impact of a good emotional appeal and as such I was not fooled into the knee jerk reaction of 'what do you need' or 'I will see what I can do'. But I had to say something. If I am not going to get sucked into the secondary negotiating stage I have to formulate a reply based on one of the primary negotiating elements of *Logic, Power or Emotion.* But which one should I choose?

I have posed that question to attendees at my seminars many, many times and smart people invariably tell me I should respond with *Logic*. And that is the classic mistake most smart people make. I understand the temptation to explain the facts, particularly if you have good facts to support your position. But I was not dealing with a factual problem. My client was using *Emotion* to make his case and if I used *Logic* in immediate response we would have had a conversation where my facts were competing with his feelings.

The key word in my last sentence was 'competing'. My facts competing with his feelings, and we all know what happens in most competitions, you end up with a winner and a loser. Never a good idea in relationship based negotiations. Let me say it again. Do not take a competitive position in negotiations unless you have no choice but to do so and clearly, in the example of my client I did not need to compete with his *Emotion*, what I needed to do was neutralize it. By responding with a position of *Emotion* I would be able to neutralize his argument instead of competing with it. As I just stated, the danger of a competitive discussion is that someone will lose and that is not a risk worth taking when the person you are negotiating with is a loved one, a friend, or in this case a valued client.

Here is how I responded to my client's appeal to give him a break on my fees because he was worried about the possibility of losing money.

I said. "I hear you buddy. I don't want you to lose money on this deal any more than I want to lose money. Let's not focus on losing money, let's look at ways that we can make this deal work for both of us, so that we both make some money".

By immediately responding to his concerns about losing money and showing some empathy for his position I was able to neutralize the impact of his emotional appeal. Having neutralized his emotions with an emotional appeal of my own I no longer run the risk of his feelings being in competition with my facts. Once I had assured him that we were on the same side and that we had a mutual goal he was relaxed enough to listen to my *Logic*. I then went on to explain to him how my fee structure was geared to attendance levels, which gave him some factual assurance on the cost and I even suggested that my being well known to his members would likely add to the level of attendance at the conference, an implied *Power* benefit to him and further assurance that using my services was a good decision for him to make. It worked. We did the deal without any price concessions on my part and with him feeling good about his choice.

I think the reason it was so easy for me to get agreement from my client in this case is that he is so good at using emotional appeals and so successful at using them to soften people up for concessions that he does not know how to respond when they don't instantly work for him. Once I had neutralized his *Emotion* he was like a fish out of water, unable to combat my positions of *Logic* and *Power*. Clearly I tried to make sure that my positions were not easy to neutralize, but nonetheless the fact that he readily agreed to my terms indicates his lack of familiarity with dealing outside of his comfort zone.

The point of this story is that *Emotion* is a double edge sword in negotiations; it might be a good choice to make if you can only have one persuasive element to work with, provided you are dealing with someone who cares about your feelings, and who is susceptible to an emotional appeal. Your children know this and they play the emotional card early and often in response to the parental power play of *because I said so*. I will explain in detail how children make that work a little later in the book. The down side to *Emotion* as a solitary persuasive element is that if the other party neutralizes your emotional appeal with one of their own you have nowhere else to go.

The important thing to remember about *Emotion* as a persuasive element is that it is a great way to soften people up and should definitely be used when your goal is to get the other party to work with you in finding a mutually acceptable creative solution. The problem with Emotion as a singular means to be persuasive is that, of the three persuasive elements: LOGIC, POWER and EMOTION, it is the easiest to neutralize. All it takes to neutralize an emotional appeal is a little empathy and an emotional appeal of your own.

To expand on that point; I remember one time dealing with my young granddaughter, who I adore even more than my own sons. On the occasion I have in mind she was about 3 years old and like all small children she only had *Emotion* to work with to get what she wanted. She intuitively realized this and would take the opportunity to cry whenever she could not get what she wanted. What I did to test my skills at neutralizing arguments in negotiations was to apply my formula to my interactions with my young granddaughter. When she started to cry because she could not get what she wanted, I did not scold her or explain to her why she could not have her way. What I did was to start crying myself.

The result was instant and amazing. She immediately stopped crying and started to comfort me. Telling me not to be sad and that everything will be ok. I know that my technique may seem a little manipulative, but what could be more manipulative than crocodile tears from a 3 year old. The point is that my experiment worked, by neutralizing her emotional appeal with one of my own I was able to get her agreement without resorting to a competitive discussion.

So, if *Emotion* is the easiest persuasive position to neutralize, the question then becomes which position is the hardest to neutralize?

Often when I pose this question to my seminar audience the response I get is that they say *Power* is the hardest position to neutralize. While I understand why my question may cause people to respond that way; let me make one thing clear, *Power* is not the hardest position to neutralize. *Power* is often the most sensitive persuasive element to deal with and for that reason I have dedicated a whole chapter to that discussion point later in the book, but it is not the hardest position to neutralize, that distinction goes to the persuasive position of *Logic*.

Chapter 4

DON'T JUST FOCUS ON THE FACTS

In 1995 one of America's most famous murder trials was played out live on national television for all to observe. I am, of course, referring to the case of OJ Simpson who was accused of murdering his ex wife and her male friend.

I studied this case closely as it was a great exercise in understanding the relative value of facts as a means to win an argument. I remember at the time that the prosecution was convinced that they had overwhelming factual evidence that would lead to a conviction. The defense, sensing that the prosecution was overconfident, set about the task of neutralizing the prosecutions *Logic* by offering alternate facts that contradicted the prosecution case. The evidence then became so confusing to the jury that it was difficult for them to determine what was true and what was not. The prosecution, in a desperate attempt to re-impose their *Logic*, asked the defendant, OJ Simpson, to try on the bloody glove that was recovered from the murder scene, without firstly making sure that the glove would be a good fit. The result of this miscalculation led to one of the most famous quotes from the case, that is: "If the glove doesn't fit you must acquit".

The point of that story is simple. Never bluff the facts.

As you may recall I asked you earlier in the book; if you could only choose one of the 3 persuasive elements of *Logic, Power or Emotion* which one would you choose? The most popular answer to this question when I propose it to attendees at my seminars is almost always *Logic*. I think the reason this is the most popular choice is that it is based on facts and is therefore likely to be the hardest of the 3 persuasive elements to neutralize.

The good news, if you selected *Logic* as your persuasive option is that it is indeed the most difficult of the 3 primary elements to neutralize, provided that what you are saying is true.

There are some important rules to observe anytime that you want to use *Logic* as the basis of your negotiation. They are:

1. Never bluff the facts. Under no circumstances should you state that something is a fact if you can't prove it, the result of a failed bluff would be that you lose all credibility at which point you have no chance of winning agreement from the other party.

2. Don't play fast and loose with the facts. Oftentimes facts need to be supported with documentation to demonstrate their validity. Always make sure that you can back up your *Logic* assertions with verifiable proof. Remember this; your fact is only a fact when the other party believes it.

3. Keep it simple. Do not sabotage your *Logic* based argument by confusing the other party with long drawn out explanations. If you do so the chances are that they will lose interest in what you are saying and miss the point of your case. Use simple to understand language and make sure that each aspect of your factual based argument is clearly understood before moving on to the next one.

A good rule to remember when presenting a written argument based on facts is: Short words in short sentences in short paragraphs.

As important as it is to ensure that your *Logic* position meets the standards I have just stated there is an even more important aspect of *Logic* to take into account, and that is to never accept at face value that what the other party tells you is true. Consider this; if you believe what you are told without verification you have, in effect, conceded the *Logic* position and given the other party instant control of fully one third of all ability to be persuasive. Always test the facts. Never simply accept them even if they appear to be true or 'make sense'. People often state opinions as if they were facts and unless you challenge them they will control the *Logic* position uncontested.

This point is extremely important when you are dealing with your children as they may have been given erroneous facts by a third party which they will then treat as true and use to their advantage in their negotiations with you. I recall when my sons were younger they would often try to persuade me to allow them to do something I was reluctant to permit. To reinforce their position they often came at me with: "But my friends' parents allow them to do it". My first response was always to ask the name of each friend concerned so that I could contact their parents and verify the facts. This quickly put an end to any attempt my sons were making to bluff the facts.

I have stated clearly that it is a bad move in negotiations to bluff the facts. It is even worse to blatantly misinform the other party as this will, if exposed, result in a complete lack of trust. This point is of particular importance in the parent child dynamic. Parents who lie to their children, casually or deliberately, should not be surprised when their child becomes an accomplished liar. Children develop most of their early behavior patterns from their parents. Good and bad.

I started this chapter of the book by stating that you should not just focus on the facts to get agreement. Sometimes we have a tendency to believe that the other party should accept our point of view simply because it is the right thing to do. As noble as that may be it is a mistake in negotiations to assume that the other party is motivated by what is right. As important as I believe it is to have control of the

Logic position I know that used on it's own it is as limited in it's ability to get agreement as both *Power* and *Emotion* are when they are used alone. The following story is a prime example of how *Logic* alone may not be enough to get agreement without concessions.

Some years ago I leased office space in Salem Massachusetts. I signed up for a 2 year lease at a very attractive price, as I think the landlord was eager to rent the space. The story begins 2 years later when I received a letter from the landlord inviting me to sign a new lease. Here is what he stated in his letter":

Exhibit A.
"Dear Barry,
Your lease is up for renewal soon and we have enclosed a new 2 year lease for you to review. We will be increasing the rent by x $ per square foot, in keeping with what other tenants in the building are paying and consistent with the going rate for the Salem area.
When you get a moment please sign and return the new lease to us"
Signed – the landlord.

The letter was simple enough. The landlord was using *Logic* as his basis for the rent increase. My first move, as I am sure you would expect, was to test his *Logic* by checking out his assertions that it was what other tenants in the building were paying and was the going rate for the area. It did not take me long to establish that he was right on both counts.

Now, if being right was the only factor in negotiations I would have signed the lease at that point and this would be a very dull story indeed. But as I stated earlier being right is not always enough to get agreement. What I decided to do was reply to the landlord to test his resolve. Obviously I could not use *Logic* to neutralize his position so I came at it from a different angle. Here is my reply to the landlord's letter:

Exhibit B
"Dear Landlord,
Thank you for the new lease. Would you please reconsider the amount you are asking per square foot. We are very good tenants, we always pay our rent on time, and enjoy our relationship with you, but cash flow is tight and we would really appreciate your help in this instance".
Signed – me.

So there you have it. I could not neutralize his *Logic* so I ignored it and instead made an appeal based on *Emotion*. Admittedly it was not a very compelling position, but what is the worse that can happen? Take a look at his reply and see what happened next.

Exhibit C.
"Dear Barry
Thank you for your letter. However, as previously stated the amount we are asking for is what other tenants in the

building are paying, and is the going rate for the Salem area. When you get a chance please sign and return the lease to us"
Signed – the landlord.

There are a couple of important points about the landlord's second letter that we should look at. Obviously he did not compromise, which frankly would have surprised me anyway since I offered very little value with the emotional appeal. He did, however, do two things badly.

1. He did not neutralize my emotional appeal, leaving it in the negotiation for me to build on.
2. He did not add any value to his first letter. Instead he simply repeated his *Logic* position.

By ignoring my *Emotion* and not adding any *Power* to his *Logic* position he has made it clear that his whole case is built around *Logic*; which, as I have said earlier is a risky decision in negotiations. He has, essentially, left the *Power* position open for me to use to build on my *Emotion* based argument.

Shortly I will share with you how I responded to the landlord's second letter, but before I do so let's see what he should have done in response to my emotional appeal. Here is an example of how I think he should have handled my letter.

He should have written something along these lines:

"Dear Barry

We appreciate that you pay your rent on time; all our tenants pay their rent on time. We understand that cash flow is tight, that is a fact of life that we all have to deal with. As you said, you are very good tenants and we like to think that we are good landlords too. (Thereby neutralizing my *Emotion*).

As previously stated the rent increase is consistent with what other tenants in the building are paying, and is in keeping with the going rate for the Salem area. (Reestablishing his control of the *Logic*).

However, if you do not wish to sign the new lease please let us know as soon as possible so that we may seek alternative tenants. (Adding the *Power* position).

If he had sent that letter I think I would have signed the lease. With a PS at the end saying. "Have you been to one of my seminars?"

As I just demonstrated all that the landlord needed to do was neutralize my *Emotion*, restate his *Logic* and insert the *Power* position and he would have given me no room to negotiate. However, in reality, he did not do any of that. All he did was repeat the *Logic* from his first letter leaving the door open for me to continue the negotiation.

For my next move to work I would have to add some *Power* to my argument, but I will need to be very careful as a clumsy power play against his strong logic would likely backfire. Here is what I said in my reply to the landlord's actual second letter: (Exhibit C)

Exhibit D
"Dear Landlord,
The amount you are asking for is more than we are comfortable to pay per square foot. If we are obliged to pay that amount we may have to consider whether or not we can continue as tenants.
We sincerely hope that you will reconsider your position as it would really help our cash flow and allow us to continue our great relationship with you. Anything you can do to help would be much appreciated".
Signed-me.

By adding an implied *Power* position and restating my emotional appeal I have added some strength to my position. I was a little nervous about adding the power play but I had a fall back position in mind if it did not work, so that I would not be left with no option but to leave.

Here is how the landlord replied to my letter:

Exhibit E
"Dear Barry,
Thank you for your letter. In view of the fact that you are a very good tenant and in consideration of your cash flow position we are offering you a rent of Y $ per square foot. (An amount half way between what I was paying and what they had previously asked for).

However, this rent will only be reduced for the duration of this 2 year lease. When the next lease is due we will expect you to pay what all other tenants are paying.

Please sign the enclosed revised lease and return it to us as soon as possible".

Signed – the landlord.

So there you have it. The landlord offered a compromise position. Which we know he never needed to do if he had handled the negotiation better at the outset. However, as much as the compromise could have been avoided by the landlord, it is fair to say that this particular compromise is well put together. Notice that he prefaced his compromise by referring to his desire to help my cash flow needs (thereby neutralizing me and gaining the *Emotion* position to his advantage). He then went on to state that this was a one time offer only (adding the *Power* position to his case). Since he already had a lock on the *Logic* argument he now controls all three persuasive elements:

LOGIC
POWER
EMOTION

At this point it would seem to make sense for me to sign the lease as there is obviously no way for me to argue with the value of his compromise. And I must admit that I was tempted to sign, but I had one more idea I wanted to explore.

As grateful as I was for the compromise offer (let's face it I didn't deserve it) I did not want to end the negotiation without testing an idea that I had developed when I intimated to the landlord that I might seek alternative space elsewhere.

To clarify, I stated earlier in this book that all negotiations are controlled by 5 elements:
LOGIC, POWER, EMOTION, TRADE, COMPROMISE. Up to this point we have explored all but one of these elements in this story. The missing element? TRADE.

Please understand that if I had no trade to offer the landlord I would have signed the lease. It would have been foolish of me to push my luck with a frivolous argument. However, I had a *Trade* in mind and it would have been a shame not to explore it. Here is my reply to the landlord's *Compromise* offer:

Exhibit F
"Dear Landlord,
Thank you for your revised offer; we really appreciate your consideration. However, I notice that you have space available on the floor above ours that is larger than the space we currently occupy. We may be interested in leasing that larger office instead if we could have it for 2 years at the rent we are presently paying. Please let us know if you are interested in this alternative offer".
Signed – me.

What I did in that letter was offer a *Trade* position as an alternative to his *Compromise* solution. The point is that a *Trade* does not jeopardize the *Compromise* offer, because if the landlord does not like my *Trade* offer I can still go back and agree to the compromise.

Just so that we are clear, my letter demonstrated the true nature of a *Trade* in negotiations because if he accepts my trade offer I would get more space and he would get more money (even using the previous rent amount because of the increased square footage).

Here is the reply from the landlord:

Exhibit G
"Dear Barry,
Thank you for your offer, however, we have just leased that office suite at the price everyone else is paying".
Signed – the landlord.

Clearly it is time for me to sign the lease. I have no positions left to play.

The point of this story is that you should not base your negotiations on *Logic* alone as that allows the other party to utilize the other positions of *Emotion* and *Power* to their advantage, even when they are unable to neutralize your *Logic*.

To summarize this chapter let me say that as much as I like *Logic* as a persuasive position; it is no more effective than either *Power* or *Emotion* without the support of the other two persuasive elements. The fact is that to be truly persuasive in the negotiating process you need to be able to use all three elements effectively, simply because you never know which one you are going to need until the negotiation begins.

As I stated earlier *Logic* is the most difficult element to neutralize because it is based on facts. However the most sensitive element to deal with is *Power* because handled badly that can cause severe harm to both negotiations and relationships. So let's take a look at ways to deal with *Power* when the other party is trying to impose their *Power* on you.

Chapter 5

ENTERING THE
CAGE WITH THE TIGER

The *Power* position is in many ways the most complex of the persuasive elements as there are, in fact, three types of power plays each requiring a different response. When you are in a negotiation and the other party makes a power play, in essence attempting to impose their will on you, it is essential to determine immediately which of the three types of *Power* you are up against. Let's start by identifying the three types of *Power* and their characteristics:

CIRCUMSTATIAL POWER
DESPERATION POWER
EGO OR AUTHORITY POWER

Let's start with *Circumstantial Power*. This type of power play typically comes in at the beginning of your negotiation and takes you by surprise. What you are dealing with here is a power play based on righteous indignation, from someone who feels they have been wronged and is looking for compensation. It is very important not to react to circumstantial power with a *Power* response of your own. All that will do is make the other party even more indignant and cause the conflict to elevate.

For example: Let's imagine you are in a work environment and you ask a usually helpful colleague to assist you in completing a project because you are behind schedule. Your expectation is that this colleague will graciously agree to lend a hand. However, instead of offering to assist your colleague says. "Do it yourself. I am sick of you asking me all the time to do your job for you". This is not the response you expected (hence it takes you by surprise) and it came in at the beginning of the conversation, which meets the other criteria for a circumstantial power play.

Clearly, in this example, there must be some circumstances that are causing your usually helpful colleague to take such an aggressive position. The worse thing you could do at that point would be to take a *Power* position of your own and say something like. "Hey, don't tell me you are not going to help. I need this project done and you are going to help out whether you like it or not!" Only bad things could ensue if you take that approach.

The best way to deal with circumstantial power is to immediately recognize that the power play is uncharacteristic and instead of responding with your own power play you should seek out the circumstances. For instance, with the surprisingly unhelpful colleague the best response to their power play would have been to say. "Is everything ok? Is there a problem that I am not aware of?" That way you avoid escalating the power struggle and instead you gather information to help you get to the root cause of the problem.

To summarize: If you encounter circumstantial power do not react with a power play of your own, but instead seek out the circumstances that are causing the problem.

The next type of power play is *Desperation Power*. This kind of power play typically comes in late in the negotiation and is a desperate attempt to avoid agreeing to your reasonable arguments. In the event that you encounter a desperation power play it is important to immediately neutralize it with a power play of your own. You should not allow desperation power to prevail.

A typical example of desperation power is when your young child is not getting their way and they resort to having a tantrum in an attempt to impose their will. If you do not immediately take control and clearly show your child that a tantrum does not work, you can expect that they will forever use tantrums as a means to get their way.

In adult negotiations desperation power is usually displayed by the other party when they cannot defeat your arguments based on *Logic* and *Emotion*. Instead of agreeing to your reasonable position or at least seeking a compromise solution, they throw in a 'Hail Mary' power play saying something like. "That's all you are going to get, take it or leave it". At that point you must not show weakness, instead you should immediately respond with a power neutralizer saying something like: "That's not going to work", and then quickly return the discussion to your points of facts and fairness.

To summarize: Never allow desperation power to succeed, because if you do it will alter the power dynamic in your relationship with the other party and they will forever know that if they bring in a power play they will get what they want. You should always immediately neutralize the power play and get back to a discussion based on *Logic* and or *Emotion*.

Finally, the most difficult power play to deal with is *Ego or Authority Power*. This type of power play usually comes in early in the conversation and is typical of the person or situation. Because this is the most difficult power play to deal with there are, in fact, three different responses that you should consider. Remember that with this type of power play you are dealing with someone who is used to getting their way or expects to get their way and they will not be easily dissuaded. Let's check out your options:

Option # 1: AGREE.
Not all battles are worth fighting. As the saying goes, "you can win the battle and lose the war". There are instances in

negotiations where it is appropriate to accept the power play being made on you. For example, if the consequences of losing the power play are greater than the rewards of winning you should consider letting it go. The fact that you did not take on the power play does not necessarily mean that you are bound to adhere to it. All you are doing is calculating that the power play is not worth contesting. What you do after you avoid taking on the power play is optional. You may accept it or you might just go ahead with your own course of action. Either way you have avoided an unnecessary confrontation.

Option # 2: FINESSE THE POWER.
This is my favorite method of dealing with an authority or ego power player. Essentially what you do with this strategy is ignore the power play and refocus the conversation. I will explain how this works, but if you really want to be good at finessing the power play coming at you then study your children, they are masters at it.

Children who have grown tired of your *because I said so* power play will introduce a new word into their interactions with you with the goal in mind of getting away from your power position and into and area of *Logic* or *Emotion*, where they may be able to get some traction in the dialogue. That new word is WHY. By asking why or why not they are attempting to refocus the conversation, forcing you to argue based on facts or fairness and getting you away from your power play. This is a very clever technique because it does not challenge your power. They know they can't say "you are not the boss of me", so they change the narrative to get you away from your control position. It might go something like this:

You tell your child to do something and instead of agreeing to do it; they say.

"Why do I have to do it?"(Attempting to move the argument away from *Power* into a fact based discussion).

Because you are a busy parent and you don't want to waste time explaining, you say.

"Never mind why, because I said so, that's why!" maintaining your power position.

Undeterred your child tries again, this time they say.

"Why do I have to do it, I always do it. Why doesn't my sister ever have to do it?" (Attempting to move you into an argument based on fairness}.

Again you resist the child's ploy and repeat your mantra.

"Never mind your sister, I told you to do it, so just do it." Hence, keeping your *Power* position in place.

Now your child responds with.

"OK, I will do it if you pay me". And the next thing you are thinking is: How much?

When that happens you have been finessed. And these are little people. They don't have any money, they can't read, they don't have great life experience, but they just out negotiated you. Be impressed.

This technique of *finessing the power* is a great way to deal with power players without resorting to a power struggle. It is a useful technique for dealing with your boss or an important customer, thereby allowing you to continue to negotiate by refocusing the conversation to either *Logic* or *Emotion*. The down side is that it is a 50/50 proposition. Sometimes it will work, sometimes not. If you really want to put an end to a power play from the other party you have to get into the cage with the tiger.

So let's look at the third option for dealing with power plays that are coming at you from an authority or ego based power player.

Option # 3: BREAK THE CYCLE OF POWER.
This is clearly the most assertive way to respond to a power play and because that is the case this technique should only be employed if you are convinced that the power play is unacceptable and that it cannot be resolved by *finessing the power*. Once you have entered the power arena there is no going back. You have to be prepared to back up your own power play. You can't end by saying "I was only joking", you would lose all credibility, and have no hope of a fair solution.

Here's how you break the cycle of power:

As soon as the other party tries to impose their will on you, you must neutralize the power play by using a sentence that equals the word STOP. You clearly don't just say 'stop', that would be clumsy and inarticulate. Here are some different ways to neutralize a power play by saying stop in a full sentence:

"That is not going to happen!"
"That approach won't resolve this problem!"
"That's not how you and I are going to get passed this problem."

Each sentence says, in essence, 'stop' and that then sets you up with the opportunity to refocus the conversation into the area of that which is right and fair. It is important to note here that you must not pause after you have neutralized the power play as that will only allow the other party time to consider how to ratchet up their power. As soon as you have used the neutralizing sentence you must immediately move the conversation onto what is right and fair (*Logic & Emotion*), making your case based on facts and fairness. It should also be said at this point; that if you don't have good arguments based on what is right and fair you should not be trying to break the cycle of power because it clearly will not work unless you have valid alternative positions to employ.

Once you have neutralized the power play and stated your case based on *Logic* and *Emotion* then it is time to pause and allow the other party to absorb the full value of your three pronged argument. They will then decide on one of three courses of action:

They will either capitulate by accepting your argument and agreeing with you (a rare but possible outcome). Or:

They will soften their position and ask you how you intend to resolve the problem. At which point you would seek a creative and collaborative solution. (I will discuss creative solutions later in the book). Or:

They will maintain a hard line and force you to back up your power play.

If you have played your hand effectively the most likely solution will be that the other party will soften and try to work out a mutually acceptable solution. But if they maintain a hard line, remember that you cannot back down now; you must follow through with the consequences of your power play.

Here is an outline of the sequence of events that I just explained:

Respond to the *Power* play with an immediate neutralizing sentence.
Follow up instantly with arguments based on *Logic* and *Emotion*.
Pause.

Deal with the response of the other party. Seeking a collaborative solution or, if necessary, by backing up your power play.

To summarize: *Power* is a sensitive area of discussion. Choose your options wisely and you will avoid confrontations and retain strong relationships based on mutual respect.

So there you have it. I have explained how to use and neutralize LOGIC, POWER, and EMOTION, the three primary persuasive elements in negotiation. Later in the book I will cover extensively how to be creative when collaborative solutions are needed to resolve problems using the secondary positions of TRADE and COMPROMISE.

However, it should be said that the 5 elements do not operate in a vacuum. If I were building a house I have just laid down the foundation. Or, if I were building a car the 5 elements are the engine, we still need to put the walls on the house or the wheels on the car. Which in negotiations means it is time to add strategies to our game plan to give it maximum potential for success.

PART TWO

NEGOTIATING STRATEGIES

"Passion may win battles, strategies win wars". - General Patton.

I love that quote by General Patton. It makes me want to be a general just so I can say it. However, it translates very well in negotiations because when it comes to doing deals "Passion" means working hard and "Strategies" means working smart. In this next part of the book I will share with you 6 strategies that will help you become a smarter negotiator and get the best possible results in your negotiations with children and adults alike.

Each strategy will be explained in order of sequence, giving you a clear road map of progression throughout your interactions with others in the negotiating arena. No one strategy is necessarily more important than any other. Each one has merits that in any given negotiation may be the most important aspect of the deal. Having said that, the first strategy just might be my favorite to discuss. Here it is:

Strategy # 1

PREPARATION

Whenever you have an important negotiation to undertake and the stakes are high; perhaps to preserve a relationship or secure a good financial outcome, then preparation is arguably the most significant strategy of all. Good preparation requires time and energy, so make sure you have the time and motivation to do a thorough job of exploring all avenues of research.

The most common mistake you can make when preparing for a negotiation is to focus too much on your own needs. The tendency is to think too much about what you could live with and not spend enough time calculating what you are up against. Many people prepare for a negotiation by calculating alternative solutions using a methodology known as, "best case, middle ground, and bottom line" preparation. They work out various solutions that they could live with before ever engaging the other party. The problem with this type of preparation is that you are negotiating with yourself and, in effect, preparing to concede. The likelihood being that once you have mentally accepted alternative solutions in your head you will quickly gravitate to any actual solution in the negotiation that fits your predetermined solution, even if it is less that you really wanted. While I respect the need to have a set of parameters within which to negotiate, don't spend too much preparation time on this aspect of the deal as it will surely inhibit you from exploring solutions with the other party that might provide a more mutually satisfying outcome.

The most effective method of preparation is to focus your energy on researching the positions of the other party. In a nutshell 'Don't prepare to concede, prepare to compete'.

Once you have your own negotiating parameters set, put them to the back of your mind and go to work as follows: Focus on the 5 elements of our game plan.
LOGIC
POWER
EMOTION
TRADE
COMPROMISE
And consider them from the perspective of the party you are about to negotiate with.

For example, ask yourself what kind of LOGIC you are going to be up against. Does the other party have facts on their side that you need to be ready for. You don't want to be taken by surprise by not anticipating any fact based arguments that you should have calculated a response to. Also ask yourself how they will perceive your LOGIC, making sure that you can back up any facts you plan to include in the discussion.

Then focus on the POWER position. Ask yourself how important this situation is to the other party. The more important it is for them to secure a deal the more leverage you have in the power position.

I want to tell you a story now that initially will appear to have nothing to do with the point I am making, but when I am finished the story it will hopefully make my point completely. Here goes:

I travel on airplanes about 100 days a year, mostly to get from one speaking engagement to another. I use these airplane trips to regenerate my batteries. It is my down time, if you will. I rarely engage in conversation with my fellow travelers, not because I have antisocial tendencies, but because I have likely been speaking all day and I need to rest my voice. Typically I will read a novel to escape the world around me, thereby sending a signal to the person in the seat next to me that I am preoccupied with my book. This usually does the trick and discourages my seat mate from too much chit chat. But on this occasion it didn't work out that way. Here's what happened:

I was sitting in the widow seat waiting for my plane to take off when a young guy who looked to be in his late 20's sat down in the aisle seat next to me. "Hi", he said. "I'm your travel partner, how you doing?"

Not wishing to appear rude I replied. "Fine, thank you" and stuck my nose back in my book, hoping that he would get the message that I did not want to be disturbed. But this guy was determined to have a conversation and he followed up with. "So, whatcha reading, something good?"

"The latest Vince Flynn novel", I replied, pointing to the cover of my paperback.

"I love Vince Flynn", he exclaimed. He then proceeded to tell me which of the Vince Flynn novels was his favorite.

Suddenly I was engaged in a conversation I had not planned on having, but this young guy was so charming and easy to chat with that I forgot my own rules and began to loosen up and before I knew it we were chatting away as if we were long lost buddies.

About 5 minutes into this impromptu conversation he asked me a question that is natural enough to expect on a plane trip. He said. "So, what do you do for a living?"

Because I was caught off guard I responded with. "I am a business coach, specializing in negotiation skills".

"Oh, great!" he exclaimed. "You're just the man I need, I am on my way to a meeting in Florida and I could use some good negotiating tips".

At that point I realized what was about to happen. I knew that if I continued this conversation I would end up giving a free seminar, and be exhausted 2 hours later. Quickly trying to diffuse the situation I said. "I'm sorry, but I really need to relax and I don't want to have to talk business".

Undeterred he continued to pressure me, saying. "Just give me something man, anything to help me get a good deal".

I knew that if I said anything to address his question now I would be locked into a long discussion that I did not have the energy for, and besides that my worst nightmare is giving a free seminar. I get paid to talk. It is not my hobby. In an attempt to end the conversation I said. "I'm sorry, but negotiation is a process and we don't have the time to discuss it effectively".

"Just give me something", he insisted. "Anything that will help me secure a good deal". He was not about to give up easily.

"OK", I said. "I will tell you the one thing that matters most in a negotiation, but that's it".

"What is that?" he asked.

I replied, saying. "The party that needs the deal the least always gets the best deal"

So there it is. If there is one thing that defines the outcome of a negotiation more than anything else it is the needs of both parties.

Getting back to my strategy of preparation. This is why it is so important, prior to the negotiation, to understand the POWER position as it relates to the other party. Simply put; the more you can determine how much they need the deal the more *Power* you will have to control the outcome. Ask yourself what you think the benefits and consequences will be to the other party and do whatever research you can to establish how much they need the deal. Remember, all you have to establish is that they need it a little more than you do and you have control of the outcome.

Continuing our theme of preparing from the perspective of the other party, the next aspect would involve the EMOTION element. Calculate your goodwill factor. The more likeability you can tap into the easier it will be to develop a trust base agreement. Be as likeable as you sincerely can in order to build trust.

With regards to the other party, however, don't be fooled here, just because someone appears likeable does not automatically make them trustworthy. Where possible research recent decisions they have made and look to see if the history of their behavior indicates that they can be trusted.

Once you have calculated what you are likely to encounter from the perspective of
LOGIC
POWER
EMOTION
You can then prepare for how the other party might engage you with the elements of
TRADE
COMPROMISE
Ask yourself what you think they might want to offer as a trade to secure a deal, or what compromises they might go to in an effort to resolve the situation.

The key message with preparation, as I stated at the beginning of this chapter, is that you should not exclusively focus your preparation on what you could live with, but that you should expend most of your energy figuring out what you are likely to encounter from the other party. Calculating how they will perceive the facts. How much they need the deal and how trustworthy they are. That way you are less likely to be taken by surprise or ambushed when the negotiation takes place.

Strategy # 2

THE DECISION MAKER

This strategy has duel implications, firstly based on whether you are perceived as a decision maker and secondly whether the party you are dealing with is truly a decision maker.

In the parent child dynamic the likelihood is that the parent has decision making powers in any interaction with the child. However, it is essential that if one parent is negotiating with the child that they know they have the support of the other parent. Children are smart, they know who the real decision maker is in the family and will often play one off against the other if they can get away with it. Parents should firstly agree with each other on any suitable solution before one of them engages the child in a negotiation. The other rule that absolutely applies to the parent child decision making process is that the parent must never make a promise or a threat in a negotiation with a child that they won't or can't back up. Nothing will sabotage the parental decision making power quicker than a false promise. Credibility is at the heart of any negotiation and once you lose it, it is virtually impossible to control the outcome of the negotiation. Children may not like the decisions that their parents make but they will respect the decision maker if they always keep their word.

This point is equally valid in adult business negotiations, but in this instance another dynamic also comes into play. That is; are you dealing with a legitimate decision maker when you engage in a business negotiation or are you wasting time on someone who has no authority to make decisions? Let's take a look at some possible scenarios.

There are essentially three different levels of decision maker interactions in negotiations. They are:

NO AUTHORITY.
This scenario typically occurs when you interact with a low level employee who has no power to negotiate anything. Don't waste time trying to influence this party as they have no authority to affect the outcome of the deal. That is why it is so difficult to negotiate deals in large department stores, because the likelihood is that you will be dealing with a clerk who has no authority. If you want to negotiate with a company employee make sure that, at very least, they fit into the next category.

AN INFLUENCER.

This party does not make final decisions but they have the power to influence the decision maker on your behalf. This person may be the assistant to the decision maker or perhaps a secretary, in which case they have direct access to the real decision maker.

There are some real advantages to dealing with an influencer, because even though they have no direct power to negotiate a solution they will have access to a real decision maker, whereas you may not, and they can potentially negotiate on your behalf. The key here is to get the influencer to want to help you, which means you have to understand what leverage you have with them. Most influencers are not affected by threats because they know that you have no direct power over them. They are also unlikely to be persuaded by promises of rewards as again you have no direct power to reward them.

The two best ways to get an influencer to go to bat for you are:

1). Get them to like you. Working on the premise that people like to do things for people they like. By developing rapport, or better still, building a relationship with the influencer you will now have an ally in the other party's camp that will make your case passionately to the decision maker.

2). Become a nuisance. If you can't get the influencer to like you, and let's face it even the most charming of people fail to allure sometimes, then the alternative is to be a pest. As the saying goes 'the squeaky wheel gets the oil'. By pestering the influencer you may wear them down enough to get them to petition the decision maker on your behalf, if only to get rid of you.

Don't underestimate the value of the influencer in the negotiating process. The fact is that they just might have more sway with the decision maker than you ever could.

THE DECISION MAKER

As all good negotiators will tell you the best way to negotiate anything is always to deal directly with a decision maker. They have the power to say yes or no instantly and can be persuaded on so many more levels than an influencer ever can. For that reason it is always a good idea to establish the decision making capacity of the other party before you start negotiating, and it could be as simple as asking them if they have the power to make a deal or do they have to report to a higher authority. If you sense that they cannot make decisions then don't waste your time trying to be persuasive, ask instead to speak to someone who can make decisions. That way you won't end up expending all your time and energy on someone who does not have deal making authority. Nothing is more frustrating in negotiations than to get to the end of a discussion only to be told by the other party that they will have to talk it over with their supervisor. Better to get the supervisor involved before you lay out your case.

This next story will demonstrate some of the real advantages of dealing directly with a decision maker and also makes some valuable points regarding other strategies that we will discuss shortly.

Some years ago my family and I were looking to buy a house. We saw a home that was newly built and unoccupied that we all liked. It was a delightful contemporary home with enough room for all of us to spread out.

Because it was a new home there was no one living in the house for me to get information from about why they were selling the property. That being the case I asked the real estate agent a few questions about the party that owned the property. She explained that the home was being sold by a financial investment company based in downtown Boston. She further stated that they were a well established small business that focused primarily on the New England market. Armed with that information I asked the real estate agent to set me up a meeting with the president of the investment company. She seemed a little taken aback by this, wondering why I wanted a meeting with the president of the company. My reason was simple; I wanted to target the highest level person who had an interest in selling the house and because it was a small company I figured that would be the president.

The strategic value for me in asking to meet with the president of the company relates to a well used negotiating maxim which is this: *The higher you are dealing in the other party's camp the more they want what you have.* Simply put, if the president of the investment company would agree to meet with me I would have gained some very useful information; namely that they really want to sell this house quickly. The fact is that the more important the person is that you are negotiating with the more they need the deal. (This also relates to my earlier point about needs analysis). Important people don't spend time negotiating deals that are not important to them.

I did not know if I would get to meet with the company's president but I did know that who they dispatched to meet with me would be a good barometer of how important this deal was to them. A couple of days later the real estate agent reported back that the president of the company was happy to meet with me in his office the following week.

This brings us to our next strategy.

Strategy # 3

CONTROL THE LOCATION

As this chapter unfolds I will get back to the story I was telling you about my meeting in Boston at the office of the president of an investment company, regarding a house I was looking to buy, because that represents a good example of controlling the location. However, this strategy is much more involved than just *where* the negotiation takes place. It also includes the need to understand that there are two other factors that have an impact on the outcome of your negotiation, i.e.: *when and how.*

WHERE, WHEN, HOW

These are the three components of the *Control the location* strategy. Let's take a look at the strategic implications of each one, starting with:

HOW

There are, in essence, three different ways to negotiate, they are:

Face to face
Telephone
Correspondence (electronic or traditional).

The first strategic decision regarding controlling the location of your negotiation should be to select whichever option gives you the best chance to secure a successful outcome. Here are the pros and cons of each one.

Face to face.
The value of a face to face negotiation is that it is the least likely scenario for duplicitous behavior. Simply put it is harder to lie and deny in a face to face negotiation than it is on the phone. If you think the other party is 'playing games' in the negotiation process then meet with them face to face and confront the behavior. Another valuable aspect of face to face negotiation is that it presents you with the best opportunity to build trust and develop empathy with the other party.

A story comes to mind that demonstrates my point about building trust and developing empathy in a face to face negotiation.

One time I was meeting with an executive of a large company that I wanted to do business with. I was met in the company's reception area by the executive's secretary who escorted me to his office several floors above reception. When we reached his office the secretary opened his door and announced my arrival.

It was a large office, and as I entered the room the executive was seated at the far end of the office behind a huge and impressive desk. I made no attempt to march into his office to shake his hand while he was still behind his desk. Like any good negotiator I know that the first rule when you meet someone you are going to negotiate with is; 'don't impress, assess'. It is better to get a read on who you are dealing with before you decide on how confident you want to appear to be.

Instead of marching confidently into his office I strolled in casually, taking in the décor. There are two strategic advantages to this approach. One is that I might see some things in his office that I can use to build rapport, such as photos, certificates or trophies. The other is even more strategically valuable and that is I will find out if he will come from behind his desk to meet me, signaling that he is going to be easy to work with, or whether he will stay behind his desk indicating that he wants to keep an emotional distance between us, and perhaps be hard to deal with.

In this instance the executive did come from behind his desk and met me in the middle of his office. As he did so I noticed a round conference table to my left side. While we were shaking hands and exchanging introductions I placed my brief case on the round table. The next thing that happened was that we adjourned to the round table and conducted our meeting in a much more collaborative fashion than would have been the case had I been stuck with sitting in the visitors chair on the other side of his desk.

The message of this story is that you should always take into account the environment in which you are going to negotiate. You can learn a lot about a person simply by observing their surroundings, which you may be able to use to build rapport. Also, you need to be aware of the seating arrangements whenever you negotiate face to face with anybody. There is a perceived power structure that relates to where people sit in a negotiation. If you are not convinced of this point consider where a judge sits in a court room.

I take this seating arrangement scenario so seriously that I often used it in my negotiations with my sons when they were growing up. There is a room in my house that was used as a study area when my children were younger. It was a place for any family member to adjourn to if they wanted privacy or just some quiet time. It also served as the location that I selected whenever it was necessary for me to discuss behavior issues with my sons.

Anytime I needed to talk with either of them I would say. "Let's go into the study for a chat". You could tell by their faces that this was not what they wanted to hear. There was almost an 'oh no, not in there' look that descended on their faces. And to compound the issue once we got in the study, if I said. "Sit over there", in a seat opposite where I was going to sit they knew this was not going to go well for them. It was almost like they wanted to say. "Dad I didn't mean it" even before I told them what the discussion was all about. Such is the power of sitting opposite the other party.

Conversely, if I wanted a more collaborative discussion where we could exchange opinions I would sit them next to me to soften the power and allow for an interactive conversation with mutually satisfying solutions. It worked every time.

To continue my thoughts on how best to conduct a face to face negotiation let me go back to the story I started earlier about my meeting with the president of an investment company in Boston about buying a house his company was looking to sell. As I mentioned before, I was pleased to be meeting with the president of the company as this indicated a 'need to sell' scenario that should work to my advantage. The downside being that the meeting was to be held in his office, where he would feel more in control of the location.

When I arrived at the office with my real estate agent we were ushered from the reception area into the company board room. As we entered the board room I immediately took note of the seating arrangements. At the head of the board room table sat a man who I took to be the president of the company and seated immediately to his right was another man whose identity I did not know, but who was later identified as the financial controller, or perhaps more appropriately as the guy in charge of selling the house.

My first thought was that the odds are three against one, not in my favor. Working on the premise that the real estate agent was getting paid a commission by the company based on how much the house was sold for. With that in mind I decided that there was one place at this boardroom table that I would not sit. That place being at the other end of the table opposite the company president. In fact what I did was seat myself in the chair next to the company president directly to his left with my real estate agent seated next to me on my left. By doing this I quickly softened the seating arrangements to make for a more collaborative and less competitive environment. The reaction of the president of the company was interesting. He seemed slightly taken aback by my close proximity and maybe even a little amused at what he took to be an obvious negotiating ploy on my part. The reality is that as a result of these seating arrangements we conducted the negotiation in a very relaxed and friendly atmosphere.

Later in the book I will tell you what happened when the negotiation got under way. But for now let me continue to explain my strategic thoughts about controlling the location of the negotiation. As I stated earlier there are three ways to negotiate. We just discussed the *Face to face* scenario; let's now take a look at the next way to negotiate:

Telephone
There are several strategic aspects to telephone negotiations that are worth exploring, they are as follows:

1). Initiate the call.
From the point of view of controlling the location it is better to make the call than receive it. The party making the call has the obvious advantage of being prepared and ready to go. In fact I would suggest that in certain circumstances it would be wise not to take a call when you know you will be in a negotiation. It might be better to let it go to voice mail so that you can analyze the message and then call back fully prepared yourself, and effectively regain control of the location.

2). Prepare as if it were a face to face meeting.
Because the telephone is such an easy and convenient method of communication there is a tendency to be casual in our use of it as a method of negotiating. In reality it is a complex negotiating tool because you are unable to see the other party and therefore unable to easily read their reactions. That being the case, always thoroughly prepare before you pick up the phone to make the call. Make sure you have a clear idea about what you are going to say and how it will be received, and have any documentation at hand that you may need to refer to. Just like you would in a face to face encounter.

3). Listen carefully.
As I just stated it is much harder to judge the reactions of the other party in a telephone negotiation. In a face to

face meeting you can more easily identify the attitude and responses of the person you are negotiating with, on the telephone you have only got their words to work with. That being the case it is essential to focus intently on what they are saying. That way you will be better able to assess the message and be in a better position to know when it is your turn to speak, thereby avoiding the pitfalls of prematurely interrupting the other party.

4). Take notes.
Note taking is an excellent aid to listening as it forces you to focus on what you are hearing instead of simply waiting for your turn to speak. Beyond that it is also a good way to make sure there are no misunderstandings. If you write down the essence of what you heard there is less chance that the other party will at some later point be able to success-fully deny that they said something in the conversation. In fact it is often a good idea to verbally summarize the con-versation at the end of the call to avoid any misunderstand-ing. In many cases you will also be well advised to put in writing the conclusions of your telephone negotiation.

The third way to negotiate is not by telephone or face to face. It is:

Negotiate in writing.
The advantage of written negotiations is that it avoids any of the possible tension involved in the human interactions. It allows you to state your case without interruption or contra-diction. There are times when I prefer written negotiations,

whether by email or regular mail as this allows you time to carefully plan your case and state your positions with clarity. All the same principles of being persuasive and creative that I have outlined so far still apply and it is important to make sure that you use good grammar and avoid spelling errors as the letter will be a reflection of your perceived professionalism. The obvious disadvantage of written negotiations is that you will not get a live response from the other party that you can counter instantly, which may lead to a delayed solution.

Continuing with my thoughts on *controlling the location*: The next aspect of this strategy is to consider:

WHEN to negotiate.

Effective negotiations require a well thought out plan and discussion. Here are a few general rules about when *not* to negotiate.

Don't negotiate when you are tired.
Don't negotiate when you are in a hurry to do something else.
Don't negotiate when you are angry or upset.
Don't negotiate when you are bored or distracted.

If it is possible time your negotiation to fit when the other party is most in need of a solution. As I stated in an earlier strategy, the more the other party needs what you have at any moment in time the greater your control of the outcome.

Finally, under the heading of controlling the location you should consider:

WHERE the negotiations will take place.

I mentioned earlier that seating positions can affect the perception of who has the power. This is also true as it relates to the physical location. Always consider whether it is to your advantage to meet with the other party in their location, your location or at a mutually agreed upon neutral location. There is no one answer to which location you should choose. It will always be case by case based on the circumstances of the deal. For example:

Choose their location if you want to get a read on the environment in which the other party operates.

Choose your location if you want to impress them with your environment. Or if you want to impose your will on them.

Choose a neutral location if distance is an issue, perhaps settling on a half way point between both home bases. A neutral location is also advantageous if you want to negotiate without anyone else being aware of your interaction.

Where
When
How

The three keys to controlling the location of any negotiation.

Strategy # 4

GET THE AGENDA

You may have noticed that the first three strategies are non verbal. They are designed to make sure that you are well prepared, that you are dealing with the right person and that you have the best possible environment and atmosphere in which to negotiate. However, at some point the conversation will begin, and the opening moves are a vital part of the strategic aspect of negotiations.

Rule # 1 Never begin with a demand or an offer. Or to put it another way, don't start at the end. The first few moments of any negotiation should be used to assess what you are up against, by asking questions to establish the positions and needs of the other party before you lay out your case.

Earlier in this book I told the story of the time my son went to play pool with his buddy instead of meeting me to go to a soccer game. When I called him on his cell phone I did not begin by demanding that he return home immediately, what I did was to ask him a gentle probing question. You may recall that I started by asking him in a neutral tone. "Where are you son?" By taking that approach I was able to get a read on his argument and then counter it with my own.

Another classic example of *Getting the Agenda* occurred during my meeting with the president of the investment company that was looking to sell a house that I was interested in buying. As I stated earlier the negotiation took place in the board room of his office in downtown Boston. Once we were comfortably seated in a collaborative style he began the conversation with the following opening move:

He said. "Barry, thank you for coming by, I am sure you are a busy man. Assume I know nothing; tell me about your interest in this house?"

This was a very impressive opening move on his part as it invites me to give him information that he can use to assess my needs, while giving away nothing of his own agenda. Fortunately for me I am very aware of the importance of getting an agenda at the beginning of any negotiation so I was ready to counter his question with one of my own.

Instead of giving him information on my position I reversed the question this way:

I said. "Richard, thank you for inviting me, I am sure you are busy too. Why don't you tell me about the house you are looking to sell and we can take it from there?"

My plan with that response was to change the discussion from being about me to being about the house. That way I can gather information without giving away my agenda early in the negotiation. Most people make the mistake of answering questions when they are asked without considering the consequences of their answer. Be careful; remember that the more questions you answer the more information you are giving away.

A good rule to remember at the agenda stage of the negotiation is this: For every question you answer, ask one of your own. By taking this question for question approach you will achieve two important goals.

You will ensure that there is a fair and equal exchange of information, thus avoiding a one sided agenda.
You will begin the process of peer level dialogue. An essential component in fair minded negotiations.

Let me explain a little more about the importance of peer level dialogue. All collaborative negotiations benefit from a climate of equality. If both parties feel that they have equal status during the negotiations there will be less need for posturing or ego driven rhetoric. The danger of one party feeling superior in any negotiation is that the other party may feel resentful and reject reasonable offers simply because their ego is bruised. As I have stated, one way to achieve equal status in a negotiation is to ask a question immediately after you have answered the other party's question. Another way to create peer level dialogue is to ensure that you are negotiating on a compatible names basis. For example; if you are using your first name you should refer to the other party on a first name basis also. If you are using your last name, refer to the other party on a last name basis, thereby ensuring that there is no implied status advantage to either side. A quick note here, you should decide strategically whether you want an informal and friendly discussion using first names or a more formal discussion using last names based on your goals in the negotiation.

To continue my thoughts on *Getting the Agenda*, some years ago I read an interesting article about a movie director that demonstrates the importance of gathering information early in the discussion and how that will determine the outcome of a negotiation.

The story relates to a movie director by the name of Brian De Palma. If you are a movie fan you may know that Brian De Palma has made several very successful movies including: "The Untouchables", "Carlito's Way", "Dressed to Kill" and "Carrie". The movie he was making in this story was "The Body Double". A favorite of late night cable TV addicts.

According to the story, while he was planning this movie Brian De Palma was driving in California when he saw a house that he thought would be good for a scene in the film.

He approached the owner and asked if he could use their house for a scene in his new movie. Stating that he would only need it for a couple of days and that he would pay them $5000 for the use of the house for the short duration of the shoot.

Now, imagine this was your house and Brian De Palma had approached you in this way. What would be your immediate response?

If your answer is to say "Yes please", then clearly you have no concept of the negotiating process.

If your answer is to say, "Make it $10,000" (or any other amount for that matter) you will have missed my point about *getting an agenda* and made the classic mistake of beginning the negotiation with a demand or an offer.

If your answer is to ask Brian De Palma a question then you are on the right track. The key here is to ask the right question that will get the best possible information that you can use to your advantage.

Here is the question I would have asked Brian De Palma to open the negotiation.

"What do you like about this house?"

The value of this question is that it puts the focus immediately on him and his needs, not yours. You will notice that I said "this house" not "my house" as it is important to avoid any personal attachment to the deal at this early stage of the negotiation. You will also notice that my question forces him to focus on what he "likes" about the house, helping to establish his level of interest and ultimately how much he wants this house in the movie.

I don't know what actually transpired during this negotiation, I only read the article. But according to the story the final deal was $30,000. Much better than the opening offer of $5,000, so I can only surmise that the owner of the house was good at getting an agenda.

I do know from personal experience that asking the right questions can be an excellent means of both gathering information and creating an agenda that slants the solution to your advantage. Let me explain:

When I first established my company in the USA, my initial goal was to generate some clients. There was a business association based in New York City that I thought might be interested in hiring me to present negotiation skills seminars to their members, so I made a phone call to set up an appointment to meet with a senior vice president of the association to discuss my services. I think he was curious to know what this Englishman thought he could do for his members so he agreed to a short introductory meeting at his office in Manhattan.

The meeting went well, I was able to impress him with my confidence and self belief and we eventually began to talk about specific dates and locations for using my services. He then asked me what I would charge for my speaking services, and I knew immediately that how I responded to that question would be crucial to the outcome of this negotiation and potentially to the long term success of my business.

My problem at that time was that I had no experience in the USA so I did not really know what I should charge for my speaking services. If I quoted him the price I had been charging in the UK I may have been off the mark with regards to the US market.

So when he asked me what I would charge for my speaking services, I paused momentarily to gather my courage and said to him:

"What do you pay your very best speakers?"

By answering his question with a question of my own I was able to avoid committing myself to a price that may have been below market value. And by asking him what he paid "his very best speakers" I was able to get him to think of me as an elite speaker, thereby reinforcing his belief that he had made a good decision to hire me.

Even if his response had been to offer me a low fee I would not have been locked into it, and by rejecting any low offer from him I would have further established that I saw myself as an elite speaker who was worth more that anyone else he employed. As it transpired his offer was more that I was expecting and proved to be a great springboard for my new career.

To summarize, GETTING THE AGENDA, is an essential opening verbal strategy in negotiations as it establishes the parameters of any potential solution. Never begin without it.

Strategy # 5

TRADE CONCESIONS –
DON'T GIVE THEM

O nce you have all the information that can be gathered or exchanged during the agenda establishing stage, the negotiation then begins in earnest. Now is the time to use the 5 Elements of LOGIC, POWER, EMOTION, TRADE and COMPROMISE to secure a deal. The key is to be as persuasive as possible using the 3 primary elements to their full extent. Not conceding quickly or easily to the other party on any important aspects of the deal.

Having said that, unless one party refuses to budge at all or conversely concedes on every point, the likelihood in most negotiations is that you will need to find a creative solution in order to secure a deal. That being the case the all important strategy of *Trade Concessions* comes into play.

Later in the book I will devote a full section to securing mutual value deals using equal value trades, as part of my discussion on collaborative deals. At this point I just want to focus on the strategic value of trading concessions.

As the saying goes, the easier it is to get something the less you value it. This is completely true in negotiations. If you give anything to the other party without getting something in return, not only will you have conceded without getting value for yourself, you will also cause the other party to wonder if they could have gotten even more from you and therefore undervalue the concession you have made. That is a terrible scenario for all concerned.

Effective negotiators know that the best creative deals have equal value concessions that give both parties something to feel good about. To make that happen, once you enter the creative stage of a negotiated solution to any issue, you need to be aware of your trading options. There are 6 trading options in negotiations. Now would be a good time to know what they are.

MONEY
TIME
PRODUCTS/SERVICES
RELATIONSHIPS
VOLUME
SITUATION

These are your trading menu items not actual solutions. The solution to a problem is secured by matching one item with another, giving equal value to both parties.

Earlier in the book I shared with you the story of the time my teenage son tried to avoid going to a soccer game by hanging out with his friend and playing pool. You may recall that he tried to persuade me to his point of view using first LOGIC then EMOTION and in each case I neutralized his position with my own logic and emotion positions. I then used my POWER to control the outcome of the discussion. In that instance nothing more was needed to secure his agreement. However, it is quite possible that a teenager will test the power of a parent and if my son had done so I would have been ready to come up with a creative solution based on the trading options. If my son had resisted my power play the hypothetical discussion would have gone something like this:

"Dad, I don't want to go to the soccer game, so I am going to stay here and live with the consequences."

Had my son taken that approach, before I implemented my power I would have attempted a trade off, saying something like this:

"Son, it is not a good idea for you to test my power as you may regret the outcome, but I don't want you to feel bad about going to your soccer game so here's what I will do. If you come home now and go to the game I will buy dinner for you tonight after the game at any restaurant you want. You pick the place".

Using the list of trading options I recently mentioned you will notice that I matched SITUATION with PRODUCT/SERVICE.

If this outcome had been necessary I would have controlled the *Situation* because my son would have gone to the soccer game, and he would have benefited from the *Product/service* of a free meal.

This is just one example of matching items from the trading menu. Later in the book we will discuss a variety of trading options in the section about securing collaborative deals.

To expand on the creative possibilities that the problem with my son and his reluctance to go to his soccer game presented, let's look at another possible way to creatively solve the problem. Let's imagine that he rejected my trade and insisted on staying at the pool hall. If that had happened the conversation may have gone something like this:

"Thanks for the offer, dad, but I just ate, so I don't need a meal tonight, so I am going to stay and play pool"

My response to that might have been:

"Listen, son, I am trying to find a solution we can both live with so that you don't have to deal with the consequences of your decision. How about if we do this. You finish playing the game you are in the middle of, and maybe even fit in one more game of pool, and then you go directly to the soccer arena and play only the second half of your soccer game"

In this scenario we don't actually trade a solution, what we do is COMPROMISE. In this example my son rejected my trade offer so we came to a compromise solution whereby he plays some pool and some soccer. This is an alternative creative solution.

To summarize this message, when it is not possible to be completely persuasive you should seek to trade concessions, and not simply reject the deal out of hand. Also, as in the example I just demonstrated, sometimes you should seek a compromise before implementing your power play. That way there can be no doubt that the power play was a fair and reasonable last resort.

Trading concessions is an important strategy as it ensures that both parties feel like they got some value from the solution. A fuller explanation of how to use all the items from the trading menu will be a feature later in the book. For now, here are some examples of how I might find a creative solution with a client who wants to utilize my speaking services but does not have the budget to pay my full honorarium.

Once I have established, through a thorough discussion that they are unable to meet my desired fee I would reduce the fee – effectively conceding MONEY – provided that they traded this concession with one of the other five trading items. Such as:

TIME
I will reduce the fee if I can present the seminar according to my time frame. Perhaps at a time when I am not busy and can fit them into my schedule.

PRODUCT/SERVICE
I will reduce the fee if they have a half day seminar instead of a full day event.

RELATIONSHIP
I will meet their budget if they invite managers from other departments in their company to attend my seminar, who would then be in a position to evaluate the effectiveness of my program for their own team members.

VOLUME
I will reduce the price if they commit to a series of speaking engagements instead of just one.

SITUATION
I will reduce the price if they pay in advance instead of normal contractual terms.

I am not sure which trading item I would use to creatively solve a problem where my client wanted a reduced price as it would always be based on the individual circumstances of each case. What I do know is that I would not reduce the price without getting something of value in return.

Having explained the value of trading concessions, it should be said that if you are not able to come up with a mutual value trade it is important that you don't simply capitulate and accept the other party's position. If you can't think of any legitimate trades using the trading menu it is always appropriate to say to the other party:

"If I do that for you what can you do for me?"

That way you ensure that you explore all possible options before moving to the final negotiating strategy, which is:

Strategy # 6

WALK AWAY

S ome years ago I saw a sign in the window of a jewelry store that read: "I WILL GET OVER THE DISSAPOINTMENT OF NO SALE FASTER THAN THE MISERY OF A BAD SALE". That saying can easily be adapted to negotiations by replacing the word sale with the word deal.

Having said that, the *Walk Away* strategy is not an end game, but rather a strategy to avoid getting into a discussion that spirals into a losing deal for you.

The reason this strategy follows *Trading Concessions* sequentially is because it is at this point in a negotiation that you will determine whether the other party is being reasonable and is trying to work with you on a mutual value solution or if they are trying to take advantage of the situation and cause you to accept a deal that is unfair to you.

The fact that there are 6 trading items (an even number) mandates that a fair deal can only occur when both parties get equal value. That is when each party gets the same number of concessions. For example: One for one, two for two or three for three. Any time one party is demanding a concession that is not matched with a concession of their own the deal begins to move into a one sided, winner loser scenario and if the potential losing party is you then that is the time to employ the *Walk Away* strategy.

Walking away strategically can be as simple as just saying no to a demand or it could be a good time to call for a pause in the negotiation to take a break and rethink how to proceed. These are just two examples of how to employ this strategy; others might be to say something like:

"I cannot make that decision right now, if we want a fast solution we will have to reject that idea."

Or

"That won't work for me, let's try a different approach."

Or

"I will have to talk that over with my partner/supervisor/ spouse and get back to you."

Or

"We are wasting our time, unless you can come up with a fairer solution, there can be no deal'

Whichever approach you select the important message here is that you reject quickly any deal that does not give you a balanced solution before the other party becomes too comfortable with it.

To reiterate: "You will get over the disappointment of no deal faster than the misery of a bad deal".

I recall a story a friend of mine shared with me about a negotiation he was involved in that demonstrated the importance of the *Walk Away* strategy. According to my friend he was engaged in a negotiation that required him to have his attorney with him at the meeting. As my friend tells it, the negotiation was not going well at the outset and his attorney, completely unannounced, got up from his seat and begun to put his papers back into his brief case. At that point the other party asked the attorney what he was doing. At which point he said:

"We are wasting our time here, this negotiation is over".

To which the other party replied:

"Let's not be hasty, please sit down. I am sure we can work something out."

This is an example of a classic *Walk Away* ploy.

PART THREE

———◆———

COLLABORATIVE DEALS

"Much has been said and written on the subject of negotiations. Books, seminars and tapes abound offering tactics and gambits to help us all become tough negotiators, or showing us how to get what we want by outsmarting the other party. The problem with this approach to negotiating is that it creates an adversarial atmosphere that ultimately leads to winners and losers. Smart negotiators focus on the more effective collaborative approach to the process, because they understand that if you try to win the other party will try to beat you. This is a dangerous game to play, particularly if you want to interact with that party in the future. The best negotiators know this and avoid a competitive style, instead focusing on collaborative solutions that benefit both parties."
- From my workshop, THE COMPLETE NEGOTIATOR.

I spent the first two parts of this book focusing on a five point game plan and six strategies to ensure that you are both persuasive and creative in the negotiating arena, thereby giving you the tools to protect you from bad deals. As important as this is, and it is very important, there is more to successful negotiations than simply winning or avoiding bad deals. We also have to know how to create good deals that benefit both parties. This is especially true when you are dealing with family members, friends or business acquaintances because in these instances maintaining the relationship may often be more important than winning. Let's now turn our focus on the four keys to creating mutual value, long lasting deals.

Unlike the six strategies I covered earlier, these four keys to collaborative deals are in no particular order. In fact, you may not always need all four keys to successfully create collaborative solutions. But one thing I do know for sure is that you will need all four strategies from time to time. So let's explore their value, one at a time.

COLLABORATIVE STRATEGY # 1

FOCUS ON THE NEEDS
OF BOTH PARTIES

During my seminars I often entertain the attendees with a little game I like to call the "Orange Test". This exercise is designed to demonstrate how often people neglect to establish the needs of both parties before rushing to a compromise solution. Here's how the game works:

In this story two people; John and Jane work for the same company. They have an excellent working relationship and enjoy each other's company. One day they meet in the company cafeteria in the early afternoon. As they are saying hi to each other and catching up on office gossip the cafeteria manager announces that she has virtually no food left and she is about to close for the day. She says all she has left is one orange which she puts on the counter and says. "You are welcome to it, free of charge".

John looks at Jane and says. "Do you want the orange?" Jane says that she does and John says. "So do I"

At this point I stop the story and ask the attendees what John and Jane should do next. Making it clear that John and Jane like each other so fighting over the orange is not an option.

Whenever I play this game the attendees invariably say that they should split the orange and each take half. An obvious compromise. And a big mistake!

By deciding that they should cut the orange in half the attendees make an assumption that John and Jane want the orange for the same reason. That is; they are both hungry. And there you have the mistake. Without doing any needs analysis the attendees jump to conclusions.

I then continue the story as John looks at Jane and says to her.

"Why do you want the orange?"

Responding to John's seemingly obvious question Jane replies.

"Because I am hungry. I have been in meetings all morning and if that orange is all there is left I would like to eat it".

Hearing this, John then says.

"Really, I am not hungry at all, I just had lunch and was on my way out when I saw you coming in and I decided to stop and say hi. But I would like to have that orange because I am putting a meal together at home tonight and I could use that orange peel as a seasoning for my meal".

I pause the story again and ask the audience if they would still cut the orange in half knowing what they now know. The answer is always that they would not.

The objective of the game is to get people to realize that we often make assumptions when we are negotiating. We often assume that the other party has the same needs as we do or, worse still, ignore their needs entirely. In this *orange test* we prove that by asking a simple, needs based question we change a quick, poorly constructed compromise into a mutually satisfying solution. Jane gets to eat the whole orange and John gets to take the peel home.

Obviously it is just a little game, but it makes a good point. If you want to solve a problem based on mutual satisfaction you need to establish mutual needs.

When you want to solve a problem with your child or with a family member, friend or business associate, and your goal is to make both sides happy, it is a good idea to start the creative part of the negotiation by asking a question like:

"What do you need?"
Or
"What would work for you?"

That way you gather useful information about the needs of the other party before committing yourself to a solution. And if the needs of the other party do not conflict with your own needs you will be able to work on a mutual value solution without necessarily having to resort to a crude and ineffectual compromise. That is the essence of a collaborative deal.

Some years ago I had a meeting with the training director at Ford Motor credit to negotiate a series of training seminars for his team in Michigan. I came to the meeting with all my selling points in mind and I was ready to wow him with my ideas. However, before I could get started on my sales pitch, this is what he said to me:

"Barry, before you tell me what you have to offer, why don't we do this. I will tell you what our goals and plans are for Ford motor credit training division over the next two years and you can tell me what you want to achieve with your business during that time period and we can see if we have matching needs".

Now that was a wow! By setting aside any competitive discussion the training director at Ford Motor Credit created a climate where we could seek solutions that work for both of us. Very impressive.

Needs analysis is at the very heart of collaborative deals. This is particularly true when dealing with the behavior and choices that your children make. Young people, just like adults, have needs and desires, even if they are not fully formed yet. When dealing with a child try to establish what their needs are in any given situation. Be it:

RELATIONSHIPS – Some children have a deep need to be liked by others. If that is the case with your child a solution to a problem may be achieved by creating social opportunities for them to spend more time having fun with family and or friends in return for doing what you need them to do.

FINANCIAL SECURITY - Some children enjoy gathering money. If your child has a need for a sense of financial security you may be able to secure agreement by adding to their piggy bank.

SELF ESTEEM - Children want to feel good about themselves. If your child has low self esteem and is acting out on that make him/her feel good about themselves. Encourage them and praise them for making good decisions. Especially if their decision is to agree with you.

FULFILMENT - If your child has strong goals and ambitions you may be able to secure agreement by giving them an opportunity to develop those goals and dreams, in return for doing what you want them to do.

REDUCE STRESS. Many children, especially teenagers, operate in a constant state of angst. Every little thing is a hassle to them. You may be able to secure agreement to your point of view by making their life a little less stressful; perhaps eliminating a chore in return for doing what you want them to do.

The purpose of these examples is to demonstrate that humans operate with a variety of needs. The key is to establish which need is prevalent in any situation that has to be resolved. If you can satisfy the needs of the other party without sacrificing your own needs then you really will be able to achieve your objective, which is; solid, long lasting collaborative deals.

COLLABORATIVE STRATEGY # 2

DEVELOP A REALISTIC SOLUTION

"Be realistic. Do not take advantage of the other party as this will risk alienating them for future deals. Don't pressure them to meet your goals if by doing so they will have to sacrifice their own goals. Conversely, do not acquiesce to the demands of the other party if they do not offer you value in return." – From my seminar THE COMPLETE NEGOTIATOR.

From time to time I present seminars in the Boston area as a means to secure corporate clients close to home. When I do that I enhance my marketing campaign by speaking at luncheon meetings for the local chamber of commerce, thereby getting the word out to local businesses in the hope that they will register attendees to my event.

On the occasion I want to tell you about I returned to my office after speaking at the chamber luncheon meeting and within minutes I received a call from someone who was at the meeting. However, the call did not go as I expected. Instead of calling to register for my seminar the caller said:

"Hi, I was at the chamber meeting and enjoyed your speech. I understand you have a seminar in the area in a few weeks and I wondered if you would be interested in advertising in my newspaper."

I should have guessed it. Instead of buying he was calling to sell to me. I imagine there were many people at the lunch meeting who were there looking to sell, not to buy.

I quickly recovered from my disappointment and invited the guy to come to my office, which was close by, to discuss the matter. During our meeting he explained to me that his paper was a free circulation weekly business publication that was hand delivered to business premises in the area, thereby guaranteeing that it would be read by my target audience. He then proceeded to quote me prices for postcard size ads, quarter page, half page and full page. That's when he lost me.

With the exception of post card size his prices were out of my league. I was not interested in a post card size advertisement that would likely not be noticed and since I could not justify the cost of a larger ad I told him I was not able to proceed. He was obviously disappointed and was about to leave when an idea came to me. I said to him:

"How about this idea, I have a four page flyer printed for my seminar. What if you inserted my flyer into your paper? That way you would not use up any of your advertising space, which you could then sell to other people while still making some extra money on my insert."

He appeared interested, replying:

"We have never done that before, but I like the idea".

"Ok, what would you charge me?" I said.

He replied:

"I don't really know, since we have never done this before. But we would have to cover the cost of our time to insert two thousand flyers into the paper. How about we charge you $800 to cover our labor cost?"

This was a very low number.

So the question is, do I take the deal? The obvious answer would appear to be yes. The benefits to me are clear; I will effectively get four pages of advertising to 2000 potential clients for not much more than the cost of a postcard size advertisement.

The correct answer is no!

Not because I don't like the deal, I really like it. The problem is that it is not *realistic* and as much as I like the deal he may come to realize that this deal is a steal for me. I pictured him going back to his office and telling his team what they were doing and telling them they are getting paid $800 for the job. At which point they tell him he is crazy to do it that cheap as it is not worth their time and energy for that price. If that were to happen I had this vision of my 2000 flyers not making it into the newspaper but ending up in the trash. Suddenly instead of getting a good deal I would be wasting $800.

Having calculated this possible scenario in my head I now needed to respond to the $800 offer. There is no chance that I will tell him to charge me more, that would go against the grain of all my negotiating instincts, but if I don't find a realistic solution that works for both of us there is a real chance this deal will go sour at some later point.

Here's what I said to my newspaper friend:

"I can live with $800, but how about we make it interesting. I will also give you 10% of the registration fee for everyone who attends my seminar as a direct result of your marketing campaign. You will have to mark the flyers I send you so that I can identify them, but otherwise no extra work will be needed on your part and you could make some good money on the deal."

This solution works on several levels. Firstly he will now have an attractive proposition to present to his team back at his office, at which point they will no longer think he is crazy. Secondly it guarantees that they will insert my flyers into the paper as they have an incentive to do so. And thirdly I will incur no cost over and above the $800 unless they add to my seminar attendance totals.

Now that is a *realistic* deal.

The objective of that story is to demonstrate that if a deal appears to be really good for you that you should reevaluate it to make sure that it is, in fact, realistic because as the saying goes; "if it appears to be to good to be true, it probably is."

Being realistic is often the most difficult collaborative strategy for people to grasp, simply because it requires looking at the solution from both your own perspective and the perspective of the other party. Nobody wants to turn down a deal that is in their favor, but unless you look at it from both sides and give it the realistic test you run the risk of damaging relationships and of the other party reneging on the deal at some future point.

I can attest to this from personal experience, because I have made the mistake of buying into a deal that worked for me without considering the implications to my relationship with the other party and it cost me dearly. It is not a lesson I will easily forget. Here's what happened:

Soon after I launched my business in America I developed a relationship with a business group that held a large conference annually for its members. I had a good relationship with several of the executives of this association and I spoke at the conference each year, which in turn enabled me to build my business. This went well until they promoted an executive, who I had only met once, to the position of President of the group. Shortly after this promotion I received a phone call from one of the executives who I was very friendly with, and he told me off the record that the newly promoted president had announced that she did not want to pay me to speak at the annual conference as she considered me part of the group, and that I should work for no fee because of the exposure that I received from the event each year.

Armed with this information I decided to contact the new president to try to dissuade her from the idea of my working for no fee. I called her on the phone and opened the conversation by congratulating her on the promotion. I then proceeded to tell her in a gentle and friendly way that my charge for speaking at the conference next year would not be increased, even though I had planned a round of price increases for my business. I explained to her that I was doing this because of the strong relationship that I had developed with her group. I hoped that by using the gambit of offering to keep my fee static that she would find it more difficult to broach the subject of my working for no fee. Thereby giving me some *Emotion* advantage as the negotiation unfolded.

What I did not expect was what happened next. Instead of telling me that she expected me to work for no fee she quickly and readily agreed to my proposal to keep my fees the same as they were the previous year. As surprised as I was at this development I made no further comment and thanked her for her agreement to my terms and hung up the phone. I should have known better.

If I had put the deal through my *is it realistic* test, while I was still on the phone, I would have realized that it was too quick and too easy. When I called this newly appointed president of the group I had been forewarned by a very reliable source that she did not want to pay my fee and yet I ignored that information. I should have realized that she was acquiescing to my fee because she did not feel confident in her skills to negotiate with a professional negotiator. I should have offered her something in return for agreeing to pay my fee. In retrospect it would have been smart of me to agree to promote her group to those companies that I do business with that might have been interested in joining her business group. Or offer to be an ambassador for her group in some other way that would have been beneficial to her. That way she would have felt that she gained something from the deal. But no, I did not do that and to this day I have never been invited to speak at the national conference for this group again.

My sense is that she resented paying my fee, even though she readily agreed to it, and as a result I gained a fee paying job, but lost a very valuable client.

To summarize: If it sounds too good to be true, it probably is. Never accept a deal with someone you have an important relationship with that is to your advantage if it clearly causes the other party to lose. It will come back to haunt you.

COLLABORATIVE STRATEGY # 3

GIVE YOURSELF ROOM TO MANEUVER

"Any time you are negotiating with a competitive individual or dealing in a competitive environment you must protect yourself from losing. It may be necessary to adopt your own competitive approach by giving yourself room to maneuver. This strategy is collaborative by result, if not by design". – From my seminar THE COMPLETE NEGOTIATOR.

If you have ever purchased a home or a car you know that some negotiations are inherently competitive. No matter how reasonable or trustworthy the agent or salesperson may sound, they are getting paid to maximize the price. We know this and compensate by being competitive ourselves, giving ourselves some wiggle room in the price negotiations.

Those are examples of obvious competitive negotiations, but we should be alert to a potential competitive situation at all times, because if we start by trying to be collaborative in a competitive negotiation we have nowhere to go but down. Simply put if you are trying to be reasonable while the other party is trying to win you will get very frustrated and likely end up losing or walking away from the deal. I see this frequently in political negotiations. Pundits talk about the need for compromise to get solutions to political issues, but if only one side is compromising, that is not a solution that is capitulation.

Be sure that you know the mind set of the party you are negotiating with before you make your move. If you know they are going to take a competitive approach to the deal then make sure that you do too.

The best and most obvious way to get a mutually acceptable compromise solution when negotiating with a competitive individual is to give yourself room to maneuver. If you need something done within a week and you know the other party is likely to resist your time frame tell them you need it today. If you want a 10% reduction and you expect resistance ask for 20%. This will force the other party into arguing against your inflated position giving you room to compromise and potentially making the other party feel good about the final solution of one week or 10% reduction.

I used this strategy regularly in my interactions with my children when they were young teenagers. If I knew they are going to resist an eleven o'clock curfew I would tell them that they needed to be home by ten o'clock and let them argue in favor of eleven o'clock. It worked every time.

Competitive by design. Collaborative by result.

The *Give Yourself Room to Maneuver* strategy is as old as time itself and is still prevalent today in many cultures. Don't ignore it, even in modern day competitive negotiations, you will lose if you do, and there is nothing collaborative about losing.

Now let's move on to the most important aspect of securing collaborative deals.

COLLABORATIVE STRATEGY # 4

AVOID SINGLE ISSUES

"The fastest way to sabotage a collaborative deal is to focus in on one issue and be inflexible. Good negotiators understand this and always keep several issues on the table as possible solutions". – From my workshop THE COMPLETE NEGOTIATOR.

A few years ago there was a writers strike in Hollywood. It got so bad that award shows were cancelled because the actors did not have anyone to write their speeches for them. I did not pay much attention to it at the time until I heard a reporter on television announce that they had reduced the problem down to one issue, and that's when I knew it was going to go on for quite some time. As soon as a negotiation is reduced to just one issue you are left with only two options, deadlock or compromise, and if one party or the other will not compromise you end up with long term deadlock. I also see this in so many industrial, commercial and sports disputes. The two sides get locked into arguing over one issue with no solution in sight.

It does not have to be that way. Not if both sides know how to effectively trade concessions

Earlier in the book I talked about the strategy of trading concessions. At the time I listed the six trading menu items and gave a brief example of how to match item for item to achieve mutual value. Now is the time to really explore the immense value of these six variable issues, as a means to achieving truly collaborative deals. They are:

MONEY
TIME
PRODUCTS/SERVICES

RELATIONSHIPS
VOLUME
SITUATION

My first big break in the seminar business came many years ago when I negotiated a contract that launched my career. It is my favorite story that I use to demonstrate the value of understanding the six variable trading items, and I would like to tell it to you now.

About two years after I came to America to start my business I still had not achieved much success. I had secured a few clients here and there but not enough to stabilize my cash flow and I was running out of money very fast. I completely underestimated how long it would take me to build a steady revenue stream and I was on the verge of going out of business. In a desperate last attempt to generate income I decided to present a seminar in my local area on how to be a persuasive communicator. I had read the best selling book "How to win friends and influence people" and figured if that is what appeals to the American public then maybe I should present a seminar on a similar theme. I bought a mailing list and had several thousand flyers printed and sent them out in the hope that a flood of people would register for my seminar and give me the exposure I needed to jump start my business. Unfortunately for me it didn't work out that way.

One week before the seminar was scheduled to be presented I had four people signed up. Not nearly enough to make it worthwhile. I was sitting in my office in Salem Massachusetts staring at my desk in despair, thinking that it was my last shot and I had blown it. Then the phone rang.

The caller said he was from the Massachusetts department of welfare. At the time my first thought was, "how did you know?"

The way things were going a couple of weeks from now I was planning on calling them!

I resisted the temptation to say anything other than. "How can I help you", and here's what he said next:

"I received a flyer about this seminar you have in the area next week, but we are not interested in sending our people to the seminar."

My thought was, "thanks for telling me", but I kept quiet and let him speak, he continued, saying:

"We have 2500 case managers here in my department whose job it is to influence welfare recipients into job training programs, and we would like to put our 2500 people through a program like this in small groups of about 25 at a time".

You can imagine my surprise. Here I was sitting in my office trying to figure out how I could stay in business and there is a person on the phone dangling the idea of 100 seminars in front of me. I took a deep breath to try and maintain my composure, and then asked the caller how he wanted to proceed. He said:

"Well I would like to come and see your seminar next week to evaluate your program".

What seminar! I had four people signed up and was about to cancel the event. Not sure what to say next I said: "Sure, you are welcome to attend". I then gave him the time and location information for the hotel that the seminar was scheduled in.

Now what?

Somehow I had to find a way to resurrect my seminar. I needed more than four people in attendance if I was going to impress the guy from the department of welfare. So I did the only thing I could think of at short notice, I asked all my friends to take time off from work to attend my seminar and to get as many of their friends as possible to do the same thing. It worked. On the day of the seminar I had 19 people signed up (15 of who were my friends or friends of my friends).

At the end of my seminar the guy from the Massachusetts department of welfare was impressed. Of course, he did not know that most of the attendees were ringers. He invited me to come to his office in Boston later that week to meet with the commissioner of welfare and discuss a proposal to train all 2500 members of his team. And that's where the story gets interesting.

I arrived at the meeting in Boston at the prescribed time and met with the commissioner of welfare and my contact from the seminar. All went well initially. We discussed the program content and the logistics of putting 2500 people through the full day seminar in small groups, over a period of 9 to 12 months. Then I quoted my price of $2000 per day, for an approximate total of $200,000 if we present 100 seminars in that time period. That is when the problem began.

They looked at each other as if confused and then the commissioner turned to me and she said:

"I'm sorry, Barry, but I thought John had told you that we pay $1000 per day for outside trainers."

I quickly went into my selling value mode explaining that with my expertise the savings they would accrue by getting people off of welfare and into the tax paying workforce completely justified the investment of $2000 a day for my program. I hoped that would be enough to sell them on my price. It did not work. What happened next only made my situation even more difficult. She said:

"Let me be clear, we don't have a problem with your price, and I am sure you would do a great job, but I thought you knew that we can only pay $1000 per day by mandate from the Governor of Massachusetts".

So now I have a problem. Nothing I can say at this point will change the mandate from the governor. I did not want to reduce my price by 50% and I certainly did not want to lose the business by walking away from the deal. If I am honest I should admit that I was sorely tempted to simply say ok, $1000 a day will be fine. Heaven knows I needed the money, and $100,000 was an awful lot of money to me at that time.

But no, I resisted the temptation to cave in and reverted to my six variables to find a mutual value solution. To reiterate, here they are again:

MONEY
TIME
PRODUCTS/SERVICE
RELATIONSHIPS
VOLUME
SITUATION

So, let's see where we are at. I wanted $2000 per pay for an approximate total of $200,000. The Department of Welfare can only pay $1000 per day for a total of $100,000. If I am going to make this deal work for both of us I will have to be able to match my concession of MONEY by gaining a concession from one of the other variable issues. I quickly calculated the options in my mind.

I thought about TIME. Would it be possible to present the seminars on my time frame, when I am not busy with other projects? This might have worked except that I did not have any other major projects and I needed to get started as soon as possible.

I thought about RELATIONSHIPS. It occurred to me that I might be prepared to present the seminars at $1000 per day if the commissioner of welfare could connect me with other department heads in the Massachusetts or New England public sector. I dismissed this because I saw it as a long shot and even if it worked the danger was that I would be locked into full time employment with government projects for years to come, which was not part of my long term business plan.

I thought about VOLUME but I saw no way to increase the seminars above 100. Maybe I could have suggested smaller group sizes for each seminar, thereby increasing the volume of seminars, but that would have extended the project way beyond the 9 to 12 month time period that was required for completion by the department of welfare.

I thought about SITUATION. Perhaps, instead of them paying me a deposit and then paying me each month as the project progressed they could pay me all $100,000 up front. That appealed to me from a cash flow perspective but would not work because of the government policy about paying in advance for projects.

Then I thought about PRODUCT/SERVICE and an idea began to percolate in my mind. Could I break down the cost of the service to increase my income from the project? Here's what I said:

"Ok, if you are locked into a maximum of $1000 per day I will work with you on that, but at that price I will have to make a $10 charge per person for course materials."

The commissioner responded, saying. "That would be ok because that would be a separate budget item."

Now the door is open. Seeing the opportunity I gathered my thoughts and came up with another idea. At that time I had just produced a series of audio cassettes on negotiation skills. One of those six pack packages that were popular with business people back in the day because they could play them in the car on the way to and from work. My tapes were not yet selling well because I had no big market to sell them to, but perhaps that was about to change. So I said:

"I think your team would benefit from some support materials that they could refer to after the seminar. I have a series of audio cassettes that I think would reinforce the messages and create a stronger learning experience. They usually sell for $59 each but if we give one to each attendee I can reduce the cost of the tapes to $30 each".

After a brief discussion with her colleague the commissioner told me that we had a deal. We shook hands and I went back to my office to prepare the contract. Let's see what we have.

100 seminars at $1000 per day = $100,000.
2500 course materials at $10 each = $25,000.
2500 audio cassettes at $30 each = $75, 000.
Total: $200,000

Thanks to my menu of variable trading items I was able to find a way to make the deal work for both of us without compromising my price.

That story demonstrates how to match one concession, in this case MONEY, with one other concession, PRODUCT/SERVICE to create a collaborative deal. This next story shows how to resolve a problem using all 6 variable issues in the solution.

Much more recently I had an office in Downtown Newburyport, Massachusetts. One of those office suites that offered shared facilities for small businesses. One of my neighbors was a partner in a firm of accountants. He and I often had lunch together and on this occasion we met at a local sandwich shop for a bite to eat, at which point he proceeded to tell me about a client that was unhappy with the cost of his audit. Here is the problem as he explained it to me over lunch:

The accountant sent a bill to this customer for audit services at a cost of $14,000. In previous years the bill had been between $6,000 and $7,000. The increase was apparently the result of the customer's bookkeeper leaving the company and the books being in disarray. When the customer got the bill they were very upset at the large increase and concerned that the accountants did not tell them in advance that the bill was going to be double that of previous years. The customer invited the accountant in for a meeting to tell him that they would not pay the bill as it stands. The accountant reluctantly agreed to the meeting, but was satisfied that the bill was correct for all the extra work that had to be done to complete the audit. My accountant friend also felt that part of the problem could be that his customer has some cash flow issues and may not be able to pay $14,000 at this time.

Having presented me with his dilemma the accountant then asked me if I had any suggestions about how he should deal with the problem. I said that I had a suggestion of my own and that was that if he buys lunch I would give him my perspective.

So for the price of lunch I came up with two ways that my friend could resolve the problem with his customer, in a collaborative fashion, offering equal value to each party.

I began by asking him what he needed to get out of the deal and he said that he would like to get paid in full and also keep his customer. A tall order under the circumstances.

Using the 6 variable trading items:

MONEY
TIME
PRODUCT/SERVICE

RELATIONSHIP
VOLUME
SITUATION

Here's what I came up with as the first possible solution.

Solution number 1

The accountant gets all $14, 000.   (MONEY goes to the accountant).

The customer pays only $6000 now and the balance at $1000 per month for 8 months, to accommodate their cash flow.
        (TIME goes to the customer).

The accountant trains the new bookkeeper at no cost to the customer.   (PRODUCT/SERVICE goes to the customer and RELATIONSHIP goes to the accountant).

The customer agrees to a 3 year contract   (VOLUME goes to the accountant)

The accountant stipulates in the contract that the audit fee will not exceed $7,000 for the duration of the 3 year contract, without getting prior agreement from the customer. (SITUATION goes to the customer).

All six variables were used in this solution. Three for each side.

My accountant friend then asked me if I had an alternate solution in the event that the customer refused to pay the $14,000 in full.

I wanted to say to him, "you're buying me lunch, not a car!" But instead I gave him this possible alternative solution.

Solution number 2.

The accountant receives $11,000, which includes the antici-pated cost of the audit of $7,000, plus the wages not paid to the bookkeeper of $4,000, because she left two months before the audit. (MONEY goes to the customer)

The customer pays the reduced amount immediately. (TIME goes to the accountant).

The accountant trains the new bookkeeper, but makes a charge for this service to compensate for the loss on the audit cost. (PRODUCT/SERVICE goes to the accountant RELATIONSHIP goes to the customer).

The 3 year "no surprises" contract remains the same. (VOLUME goes to the accountant and SITUATION goes to the customer).

Having offered him two solutions to his problem I finished my lunch and wished him luck at his meeting with the customer.

Just incase you are interested; the customer refused to pay the $14,000 and agreed to solution number 2.

What both these stories demonstrate; the Massachusetts department of welfare and my accountant friend is that when you utilize your variable trading options there is usually a collaborative deal to be found. It is when you get stuck arguing about a single issue that negotiations tend to stall.

I would highly recommend that you work on collaborative solutions any time you are dealing with family or friends. If you take advantage of the other party simply because you can it will inevitably take a toll on your relationship. As a married man I realized this early on in my relationship with my wife. My skills as a negotiator would allow me to take advantage of her kind nature, but at what price? I don't want to end up in a one bedroom, furnished apartment!

Securing collaborative deals with your children is also important to the long term impact of your relationship with them. As tempting as it may be to say *because I said so* eventually they will resent your one sided approach to problem solving and become combative. The earlier you can begin to work with your children on mutual value solutions the stronger your relationship with them will become.

PART FOUR

EVERTHING ELSE
YOU NEED TO KNOW

So far I have covered the five elements that control the outcome of all interactions. I have shared with you the six strategies that will protect you in your deals with others, and I have given you four strategies to secure mutual value, collaborative deals in relationship driven negotiations. Now let's take a look at some of the other components to being an effective negotiator with both your children and with grown ups.

THE CONFIDENCE FACTOR

"The most effective negotiators have a strong sense of self belief and confidence in the goals they are striving to achieve in negotiations"- From my seminar the COMPLETE NEGOTIATOR.

In negotiations, as in life, a confident and engaging personality will serve you well. In fact, in my experience confidence has two profound benefits: Firstly, confidence makes you more persuasive. Simply by exuding self belief and an aura of confidence you will get people to pay attention to your point of view, and getting people to listen to what you have to say is a strong component of being persuasive. There is something very engaging about a confident personality that people admire and are drawn to and provided it does not cross the line into obnoxious arrogance it will serve you well in negotiations.

The second profound benefit of feeling confident is that it reduces and even sometimes eliminates stress from the situation you are dealing with. Stress, for me, is a sense of despair caused by feeling out of control. When events are overwhelming and you cannot control what is happening there is a very strong likelihood that you will feel stressed and therefore act irrationally, which can have a profoundly negative effect in problem solving.

Let me put it this way: If stress is the sense of feeling out of control, then confidence is the sense of feeling in control. Ergo confidence eliminates stress.

Developing confidence in your ability to manage a situation requires a laser focus on three questions. If you can answer yes to each question you will have the confidence to engage and resolve any problem that confronts you. Let me make it clear, however, you cannot fake this. You must be able to genuinely answer yes to each question, even if it means delaying taking on the problem until you have each "yes" answer in place.

So, let's take a look at the three questions that will determine your level of confidence. They are:

1. DO I KNOW WHAT I AM DOING?

Answering yes to this first question is an essential part of being a confident negotiator. You need to fully understand what you are dealing with in order to achieve your goals. In face to face negotiations, particularly those involving children or family members, it is important to establish the facts before seeking a solution to a problem. Often in negotiations involving family members, emotions and desires drive the other party's position and you need to get past that by asking fact based questions and by gathering information on all sides of the situation in order to establish a basis for a solution.

Knowledge is at the heart of a confident personality and is central to being ready to confidently negotiate in all aspects of life. In this modern world of internet access there is no excuse for lack of research. Whether you are buying or selling a vehicle or a house there are numerous web sites that will give you relevant information to ensure that you are well prepared and knowledgeable on all aspects of the deal. The same is true for business transactions. All companies have web sites that will give you an insight into their business dealings, and by using a search engine you may also be able to find out more about the other party by running a search of the name.

Whatever the nature of your impending negotiation take the time to gather as much knowledge as possible before you engage the other party. There is no substitute for information as a confidence builder.

2. CAN IT BE DONE?

The second question you will need to be able to answer "yes" to, is not about what you know but more about your ability to follow through. In the case of a major product purchase it would entail making sure that you have the financing in place before you make an offer. In the case of a negotiated settlement of an issue with your child it would be making sure that you have the support of your spouse or partner before making a commitment to a solution that involves the family. In a business transaction it might involve making sure that you have the support of your boss or coworkers before you make a promise to a customer.

I like to refer to this aspect of confidence building as establishing your support system. No matter what the nature of your potential negotiation is you need to know that you can do what you plan to say you are going to do. Nothing will destroy your confidence faster than having your decision overturned by someone else or discovering that you don't have the resources in place that you thought you had.

3. DO I WANT TO DO IT?

This third question is the most important one to answer "yes" to because it speaks to your level of motivation and without the required motivation you will not take the time to make sure you have the first two questions adequately answered. Let's face it, if you don't care enough about the outcome of your negotiation you won't have any interest in establishing the full knowledge you will need to confidently engage the other party and you won't care whether you have a support system in place. If the outcome of any given negotiation is not important to you then you probably shouldn't be doing it anyway. If it is important then finding your motivation is essential.

By asking yourself the question "do I want to do it", you will begin to determine your true level of motivation. You can also ask yourself other motivation related questions, like: "What do I hope to gain from this?"

Or "What problem will this negotiation solve?"

Or "what difference will this make to my life?"

Once you have visualized the positive outcome of getting a deal you will then be motivated to achieve it. One word of caution here, as important as it is to be motivated to confidently engage in negotiations, it is also important not to get excitable when you are negotiating as that may cause you to lose your focus on a fact based solution. More about that later, for now I want to elaborate on how to be fully motivated whenever you need to be.

In negotiations, as in life, motivation is the engine that drives the solution to all problems. Truly motivated people see opportunity in every problem and a challenge in every difficulty, but being motivated is not something that you achieve accidentally, it is something that you achieve by following a strict discipline. That discipline is:

BECOME RESULTS DRIVEN, NOT TASK DRIVEN.
Or to put it another way; focus on what you are getting out of it, not what you are putting into it.

Let me give you an example. I travel extensively in my business, often spending 3 or 4 days a week traveling through airports and flying from city to city. As any regular air traveler will attest there is no joy in modern air travel. Even if you travel first class you still have to deal with security lines and potential delays and flight cancellations. For most people the misery is compounded by having to travel coach class where the experience is akin to being herded in a cattle truck. As I often like to say about flying: On a good day it is a bus in the air. On a bad day it's not in the air. The point of this story is this, people often say to me in casual conversation that they don't know how I can stand to fly so much with all the frustrations that flying creates, and I always tell them the same thing. It is not a problem for me because I don't think about it. It is a task, and I never focus on a task unless it is inherently enjoyable.

The problem of thinking about any task that you do is that you will take on the mood of the task you are doing. If the task is boring and you are thinking about it you will soon become bored. If the task is frustrating and you are thinking about it you will become frustrated. If the task is tiring and you are thinking about it…. Well, you get the point.

Thinking about tasks is almost always counter productive to being motivated. In fact thinking in general is over rated, causing people to suffer from the condition known in medical circles as paralysis by analysis. If you know what you are doing (because you planned effectively in advance) and if you have a good support system in place, there is no need to over think it. Focus on the results, think about what you are getting out of it and that will sustain your motivation, even during the most onerous of tasks.

There are a couple of stories I like to tell about the power of being motivated. One is a business example and the other relates to one of my sons. Let's start with the business story.

Many years ago, in my previous life, I was promoted to credit manager at Hertz Rent a Car in London. At the time I was the youngest member of the Hertz head office management team, with a staff of twenty people to motivate. Our primary job was to ensure that our corporate customers paid their bills to us on time, and when they didn't to call them on the phone and encourage them to pay that day. I was aware that the team was not highly motivated, having been part of that same team before I was promoted, so I decided to try something a little different to raise the level of motivation. I gathered the team together and announced that I was going to come in half an hour earlier each day. That did not sit well with the team who initially thought that they would also have to come in early. I quickly allayed their fears by explaining that I wasn't planning on starting work a half hour early, but, that what I was going to do was get a cup of coffee then head over to the mail room each morning and scope out any checks that had been received that day. I said that it was totally voluntary but that if anyone wanted to join me they were very welcome to do so. Initially it was just me and one staff member who wanted to impress me with his loyalty, but within 2 weeks every member of my team was coming in early to be part of the fun, and we really were having fun. We would meet in the mail room, shoot the breeze about the night before and check to see which customers had sent payments that day. High fiveing each other and generally celebrating our successes. By the time we hit the desk half an hour later we were pumped and fired up to contact any customers who had not yet paid. Why? Because we had just spent the previous 30 minutes focusing exclusively on results.

As a foot note to this story I should tell you that 2 months later I got a memo banning us from the mail room. Apparently we were too disrupting to the people sorting the mail. Nonetheless the exercise served its purpose, my group became results driven and I now had a much more motivated team who went on to improve job performance considerably that year.

This next story is much more recent and is my favorite story about the power of motivation. The story begins in 2002 and ends 6 years later in 2008.

In 2002 my youngest son Scott was a senior in high school. He was not a particularly studious young man, and his grades were average at best. He decided that he did not want to go to college because in his mind that would just be four more years of boring academic study, which had no appeal to him whatsoever. My concern was that without higher education he would be entering a competitive job market at a disadvantage and I shared that with him. Undeterred he informed me that he was going to join the United States Air Force and train to become a part of the USAF military police, with a 6 year commitment.

I clearly had mixed emotions about this. On the one hand I was very proud of him for wanting to serve his country in our time of need (this was 2002 after all). On the other hand he was potentially signing up to put himself in harms way and as a father that gave me some anxiety. He went through basic training in Texas and was eventually assigned to guard nuclear weapons at Nellis air force base in Nevada, which happens to be very close to Las Vegas. This also gave me some anxiety as Las Vegas is a risky place for a young man to spend his leisure time.

All went well initially, he was excited to have high level clearance to guard the nuclear weapons facility, even remarking to me at one point that he had the power to shoot a general if he refused to halt on demand. I smiled at that thought and told him not to shoot more than two generals as that would probably not be good for his career.

The problem began about 3 years into his job when he became completely bored with the monotony of spending his days checking ID's. Since he had signed up for 6 years of service this needed to be addressed. After some deliberation he decided to transfer to the air traffic control section of the air force and was sent to Biloxi Mississippi to learn how to do that. Some weeks later my wife Kathy informed me that Scott was about to graduate from the Air Force air traffic control school and that we needed to go to Biloxi for the graduation ceremony. Frankly, I wasn't excited about taking time out of my schedule for this because I suspected that he would get bored with this job quickly too and soon be looking for another transfer. However, my wife was insistent that I attend, which meant that I was going anyway, regardless of my misgivings.

I recall the graduating ceremony as clearly as if it were yesterday. There were about 70 people seated in the room, mostly family members of the graduating class, and also several friends in dress uniform seated at the back of the room to observe the proceedings. There were 12 students graduating that day, lined up along one wall waiting for their names to be called by the senior officer who stood at the front of the room at a podium. One by one the graduating students were called by name and they marched to the podium to receive their diplomas. My son was standing midway in the line of graduates and my wife and I waited patiently for his name to be called.

"Next up" announced the senior officer. "Is Scott Elms who achieved the highest score in the class of 97% ".

There was an audible gasp of surprise from the people seated in the room, mostly from me. I looked at my wife and said to her. "Did you know this?"

She smiled and replied. "Yes I did".

"Why didn't you tell me?" I asked and she replied. "Because I wanted to see your face when you heard it".

For the next few minutes I waited impatiently while the rest of the graduates received their diplomas, anxious to talk to my son about this amazing feat. I was dumfounded about how he went from having no interest in academic studies to top of his graduating class at air traffic control school.

Eventually the ceremonies concluded and my son made his way over to my wife and I wearing a big self satisfied smile on his face. I gave him a big congratulatory hug then looked him in the eye and said to him: "How did you do that?"

He replied. "Dad, I found out that air traffic controllers in the commercial world can earn $150,000 a year".

Translation; he found his motivation.

The two stories I have just told you are examples of motivation as it relates to life in general, but the value of motivation is equally important when dealing with negotiations specifically. Focus your mind around the positive impact of securing a deal. If you never take your eyes off the prize you will attain the motivation you need to see it through with determination and resolve, no matter how difficult the task may be.

Remember the 3 keys to being a confident negotiator are:

Knowledge
Support System
Motivation

Because, when you know what you are doing, have a support system that allows you to do it and you want to do it, you are truly ready to make it happen.

SILENCE IS GOLDEN

A wise man once said; you have two ears and one mouth, use them accordingly. Good advice indeed.

One of the most valuable things you can ever do in negotiations is to simply be quiet and let the other party talk. Most people are uncomfortable with silence in negotiations and will fill it with words. Let that be the other party. The more they speak, the more you learn. I have been in many negotiations where the other party talked themselves into my deal all because I did not interrupt them, allowing them to come around to my way of thinking all on their own.

There is a saying in sales that people love to buy, but hate to be sold to. The same principle applies to problem solving in negotiations. People want to resolve issues they just don't like to think that they are being pressured into someone else's solution. If you remain silent and let the other party work out the value of your ideas on their own they are more likely to feel ownership of the solution and be more satisfied with the outcome.

Occasionally people also just need to vent their frustrations. Sometimes remaining quiet and letting them get it off their chest may be all you need to do to calm them and refocus the conversation on solutions instead of problems. I learnt the value of this technique when I worked as a customer service representative. Often a frustrated customer who was allowed to vent their frustrations would conclude their tirade with an apology for taking it out on me and offer a thank you to me for letting them have their say, when all I really did was stay silent. Most people instinctively know when they are being irrational and are grateful to you for not pointing it out to them.

The problem with my suggestion that you keep quiet and let the other party talk is that it is hard to do. The temptation to inject your own point of view is almost irresistible in any discussion, particularly when the stakes are high. The key to success by being quiet is to learn to be an active listener. Concentrate on what they are saying, don't let your mind wander. Take notes where appropriate and if necessary inject verbal prompts into the conversation, such as: "OK" or "what else" or "tell me more". You can also use visual prompts to encourage the other party to keep talking, including making eye contact and nodding occasionally while they are speaking. Whichever technique you use to stay focused is entirely up to you, but it must be sincere and reflect a genuine desire on your part to hear what they have to say, otherwise you may come across as patronizing or condescending which is obviously counterproductive to getting agreement.

CONTROL YOUR EMOTIONS

I spent a lot of time earlier in the book talking about the importance of developing an emotional connection when negotiating, recognizing that people like to do things for people they like. Now I want to talk about the pitfalls of out of control emotions and the need to avoid them.

PLAY IT COOL
Firstly, I want to focus on the danger of being too excitable or exuberant in negotiations. While I admire enthusiasm as a personality trait, it can be a potential liability when trying to reach agreement. The more you appear to want something the more likely it is that the other party will exploit your excitability to their own advantage. Play it cool, keep your enthusiasm in check as it relates to your needs and only show enthusiasm when explaining the benefits of a solution as it relates to the other party, as a way to get *them* excited. This is a tactic that I highly recommend when you are buying a car, a home or any other product where

the price is negotiable. Don't fall in love with the product, or at very least don't show your emotional attachment to it thereby enabling the other party to exploit your needs and desires. Keep your excitement to yourself, it will serve you well.

REMAIN CALM
Secondly and in many ways, more importantly I want to talk about remaining calm and composed when the other party shows anger or frustration in a negotiation. This can be very difficult to do in the heat of a discussion, because as the saying goes: The attitude you get is the attitude you give back. All our instincts tell us to respond in kind. The real skill is in the ability to absorb the frustration and anger displayed by the other party and respond in a calm and calculated fashion. It will be very difficult for the other party to remain hostile if you are not.

I am reminded of a conversation I recently had with my neighbor. We were shooting the breeze about life in general while sharing a drink on a hot summer afternoon when he mentioned that his young teenage daughter was upset with him because she felt he was too strict with her about the amount of time she was allowed to use the computer for social networking. In her frustration she yelled at him that she was going to run away from home. He told her calmly that that was ok, provided she was back by 9.30pm because she had school the next day. That made me smile.

Not all emotional outbursts are that easy to handle, however, and this next story illustrates just how tough it can be to remain calm when faced with an emotional issue.

Part of my preparation for the training program with the Massachusetts Department of Welfare, which I talked about earlier in the book, involved doing some research on conflict management. I was asked to observe a meeting where a group of people were getting together to discuss dealing with the verbal assaults that they received from Family members who had anger management issues. It seemed like it would be a good way for me to familiarize myself with the possible conflict issues that Welfare managers might encounter with some frustrated welfare recipients so I was happy to attend.

The meeting lasted 45 minutes and proved to be one of the most valuable experiences I have ever had. During the session I sat at the back of the room and took notes as the participants split into 2 groups to discuss the emotional distress they were dealing with. The groups comprised of mentors on one side, those who had extensive personal experience in this area, and on the other side the folks who were newly embroiled in the conflict. As I observed the discussion a theme quickly began to surface.

One of the less experienced attendees was articulating a problem when she was abruptly interrupted by one of the mentors who said.

"You have got to get out of the movie".

At first I struggled to understand the relevance and context of this observation as it appeared to have nothing to do with managing emotions. Then I heard it again, and again.

"You have got to get out of the movie".

It soon became a mantra that dominated the meeting.

After about the third time I heard the expression I began to realize the significance that it had in controlling emotions. What the mentors were illustrating with this expression was the importance of emotionally distancing yourself from the outburst by the other party. By saying 'get out of the movie' they were essentially saying exclude yourself emotionally from the performance you are hearing from the other party. A metaphorical stepping out of the movie and into the audience so that you can observe and analyze the behavior without being embroiled in it.

By the time I left that meeting I had learned a valuable life lesson, and now, whenever I am confronted by an emotional outburst I say to myself. "Get out of this movie". It really has helped me maintain my emotional equilibrium and allowed me to evaluate each emotionally charged issue dispassionately.

It would seem obvious that if you respond to an uncontrolled emotional outburst with one of your own you run the risk of losing control of the situation, possibly saying something you will regret later. Yet most people make this mistake from time to time and it rarely ever ends well.

I am reminded of the time that I had a contract to work with Ford Motor Credit to train the team that was responsible for negotiating with customers who had not maintained monthly payments for the car that they had purchased and as a result subsequently had the vehicle repossessed. After the car was sold at auction a bill would be sent to the customer for the amount still due to be paid after deducting whatever was received at the auction. This often amounted to several thousand dollars which the team at Ford Motor Credit was responsible for collecting from the customer. As you might imagine this presented a difficult challenge as they were dealing with people who could not pay $200 or so each month, and now were being asked to pay several thousand dollars for a vehicle that was no longer in their possession.

As a prelude to my training program I spent several days listening to and observing the team as they engaged customers on the telephone. I was not at all surprised that many customers behaved angrily and emotionally during the phone call, what bothered me was that occasionally the representative from Ford Motor Credit responded to the customer's outburst by also reacting angrily and emotionally, quickly causing the conversation to degenerate into a contest about who could yell the loudest and often ending with one party or the other slamming down the phone to end the call. Leaving everyone concerned feeling emotionally drained and with no resolution to the problem at hand.

The point of this story is simple. If you don't control your emotions you will likely end up in a heated argument that has nothing to do with finding a solution to the problem you are trying to resolve.

To summarize; keep your emotions in check, do not get excitable or show frustration when trying to solve a problem with a child, a family member, a friend or a business acquaintance. No good can come of it and relationships can sustain long term damage as a result.

IT'S NOT WHAT YOU SAY, IT'S HOW YOU SAY IT

Communication experts tell us that 93% of the impact we have when we communicate with others is non verbal. In fact, I recently saw a study that stated it this way:

Visual   55%
Vocal   38%
Verbal   7%

If those numbers are accurate we better take into account what we look like and what we sound like as well as what we say when we negotiate with others.

I was in a department store recently buying some clothes when I observed a mother and young daughter waiting in a long check out line. The little girl who was probably about 5 years old was restless and fidgety so she began to dance around in the line, occasionally moving away from her mother as she performed her dance moves. This irritated the mother whose patience was tested by waiting in the long line and having to constantly keep an eye on her young daughter. Several times the mother called out to her daughter, telling her to stop dancing around and to come and stand by her side. The little girl appeared impervious to her mother's pleading and continued to dance around obliviously. As her frustrations grew at being ignored by her daughter the mother began to raise her voice and make threats about potential punishment for not doing as she was told. As each threat was ignored the impatient mother raised her voice even louder until she was close to screaming at the little girl. Eventually she became so frustrated by her daughter's behavior that she stepped out of line and grabbed her daughter forcibly by her arm and returned her to the line where she yelled at her some more, causing the little girl to start crying in the store.

As I watched this scenario play out I thought to myself how much less stressfully this could have been resolved if at the outset the mother had calmly stepped out of line and knelt down in front of her daughter, made eye contact and told her gently to stop and then taken her back in line and held her hand. Another option would have been for the mother to step out of line, pick up her daughter and make eye contact while smiling at the little girl and then return her to the line.

My point is this. Verbally assailing someone who is not responding to your ideas almost never works effectively unless it is accompanied by an appropriate visual and vocal message. Yelling idle threats only adds to your level of frustration and causes the other party to tune you out.

As a parent and as a professional negotiator I am acutely aware of the importance of using all aspects of communication to my advantage as a means of securing agreement. Let's take a look at how to maximize our impact visually, vocally and verbally. Starting with:

VISUAL

If you are not convinced that visual aspects of communication are more impacting than the words we use then visualize this scene. You are walking alone on an empty street on a dark night when a stranger approaches you, points a gun at you and says; "give me your money". Working on the assumption that you are not Batman my guess is that you would give the robber your money. My question is; was it what he said or the sight of the gun that would cause you to part with your money?

Here's another example. I remember one time asking my then teenage son who was lying on the couch what he was going to do with his life and he replied:

"I have big plans Dad".

At which point I said: "Yeah, maybe, if you ever get off the couch".

What am I more likely to believe, what he says or what I see?

The concept of visual communication plays a big part in successful negotiations. Where you sit or stand in relationship to the other party can have a profound effect on the outcome. In my experience the most combative form of visual communication is to stand opposite somebody, followed by sitting opposite. Conversely, sitting side by side or adjacent to each other creates a more collaborative environment. Depending on your goals in each negotiation you should choose accordingly.

If you want to maximize your combative posture then stand in front of the other party while they are seated. This technique is common in interrogations.

If you want to present some ground rules for behavior then you should choose to sit opposite the other party, perhaps in a higher chair. This technique is common in a court of law.

If your goal is to discuss a solution to a problem that benefits both parties equally then you will create a more relaxed environment if you sit side by side, thereby avoiding the hard visualization that results from face to face across a room.

Let me start this next story by saying that I love my wife dearly, but.....when we go out to dinner, and it's just the two of us, I prefer to not sit opposite her at a table or a booth. My concern is that as the evening wears on the direct face to face eye contact will cause her to direct the conversation to some issue that she wants to resolve and that we will end up in a combative discussion. My thinking here is that if I have to have an issue driven conversation with my wife I want it to be at a time and place of my choosing and not face to face across a table over dinner. To minimize the likelihood of combative discussion and to create an environment where we can just enjoy each others company, while having a relaxed conversation, we choose to sit next to each other at the bar. We even do this in fancy restaurants. It works every time.

I made a point earlier about eye contact in my story regarding the distraught mother in the department store. Stating that the best way for her to get the attention of her daughter was to kneel down and talk to her eye to eye or to pick her up and look her in the eye. This is arguably the most impacting aspect of visual communication and I would argue that direct eye contact should be used whenever you want to make a point forcefully in your negotiations with children, or with adults for that matter.

There is, of course, more to visual communication than seating positions and eye contact; it also encompasses body language and grooming. Having said that, visual communication should not be confused with *dress for success*. This is not about making a fashion statement or trying to impress someone with your wardrobe choices for career advancement purposes; this is about having a visual image that is consistent with your words. If what you are wearing is a distraction then it is likely that your words will not be heard. If you look like a clown but sound like a scholar the clown image will prevail.

VOCAL

Perhaps the most underestimated aspect of communications is the sound of your voice. If you speak too loud or too softly your message will be lost. If you sound bored or distracted the other party will lose interest in what you are saying. If you mumble or stumble over your words you will sound unsure of yourself causing the other party to disengage from your message. There are a myriad of ways that the sound of your voice can distract from your message. Here is one example:

I recall one time I was flying from Boston to Atlanta on business and because of equipment failure and a change of planes the passengers were asked to speed up the boarding process by ignoring their seat assignments and taking any available seat. This worked out fine until just before the plane was due to take off, then at the last minute a group of 10 or so Japanese travelers boarded the plane. They had just transferred from a connecting flight and were unaware of the open seating arrangement. They quickly became confused when they saw people sitting in what they thought were their assigned seats. Nearby passengers tried to explain to them that they should sit in any available seat, but because of the language barrier and the natural tendency the Japanese have for polite behavior they resisted taking what they assumed to be someone else's seat. Passengers continued to gesture to the confused group, even using hand signals where words were not working. Still the Japanese contingent continued to look around in a confused state, further irritating the passengers who were trying to get them to take any seat. Then, because all else had failed, several fellow passengers began yelling loudly at the Japanese group in English. I guess the thinking here was that if they don't speak the language then yelling in the same unfamiliar language will work. It did not; it just made the Japanese travelers more confused and did nothing to alleviate the problem. Fortunately a flight attendant came to the rescue and seated the confused passengers before a full scale riot occurred.

The moral of this story is that raising your voice does not improve your message.

Other vocal mistakes include: Speaking too fast, as that sends a signal that you are nervous. And speaking too slow or in a monotone voice as that will quickly cause the other party to lose concentration and stop listening to what you have to say.

The key to good vocal communication is to project an energetic tone. The principle here is that if you don't sound interested in what you have to say, don't expect anyone else to be interested in your message. Be vocally energetic, this is a major component to being persuasive in the negotiating process.

This brings me to the third aspect of communication, which is:

VERBAL

My belief is that if you master the skill of visual and vocal communication then what you say will be heard loud and clear. So make sure when negotiating that you have a good command of the words you are using.

When I first moved to the United States, back in the mid 1980s I was accustomed to speaking British English, which I soon discovered was different from American English in a multitude of ways, some subtle and some quite extreme. I had only lived in the Boston area for a couple of weeks when I was reminded of those differences. One of my neighbors at the time asked me if I wanted to car pool to work as our offices were close to each other in a nearby town. That seemed to me to be a good idea so I said. "Sure, what time do you want me to knock you up in the morning?"

I think he said something about getting the train instead. In my defense I was speaking British English, whereby knock-ing someone up means literally knocking on the door. In the USA apparently, knocking people up has a whole dif-ferent meaning. Suffice to say I have made the adjustment.

Being aware of whom you are speaking to and selecting your words appropriately is a central part of being an effective negotiator. The ability to relate and connect with another person emotionally can be as simple as the words you use.
170

And to this end I have a simple formula that I like to use to ensure that I am heard and understood at all times. That is:

Speak with conviction and avoid confusion.

Let's start with speaking with conviction.

Good negotiators know that strong words suggest strong resolve. When you want someone to accept your ideas it is advisable to avoid the language of debate and speak the language of decisiveness. For example, using words like 'definitely' and 'absolutely' suggest a clear sense of self belief, whereas words like "hopefully' and 'maybe' has the opposite effect.

My first life experience of the value of word selection happened in grade school. I recall having a crush on my French teacher and as a result I took every opportunity to get her attention in class. She was completely oblivious to my school boy crush, but was kind enough to indulge my efforts to get her attention. On one occasion she was reviewing an essay that I had completed and, much to my dismay was critical of some of my work. She scored a line through several parts of my essay saying that I had missed the essence of the character I was writing about. I looked at her and said boldly.

"Do you really think so?"

To which she replied. "I don't think so, I know so!"

This quickly put an end to that conversation.

I learned a valuable lesson that day, which is that if you don't want a debate use words that leave no doubt about your position.

Now, let's take a look at avoiding confusion.

It is very difficult to be taken seriously in a negotiation or in any aspect of communication when the other party is confused by what you say. Here are a few things to remember if your goal is to be heard and understood:

Don't use slang words unless you know for sure that the other party is familiar with your slang. My earlier example of car pooling with my neighbor is a good case in point.

Don't start a sentence you don't know how to finish. Nothing will make you sound more indecisive than "um" and "Ah" and "you know" peppered throughout your message.

Don't use buzz words or trendy language in excess as this will irritate the other party to the point of distraction.

I was reminded of this last point some years ago when I presented a series of negotiation skills seminars for the Federal Reserve Bank of Boston.

On the first morning of the first seminar I was a little apprehensive because I knew I was dealing with very knowledgeable and serious people and my speaking style tends to be loose and irreverent. My goal is to amuse and entertain as well as inform my audience, which can be a challenge when dealing with serious minded bankers.

By the time we adjourned for lunch I was very concerned that none of my attempts at humor had elicited the desired smiles and laughs and I resigned myself to the fact that this was not going to be a fun day. During the lunch break the senior manager in the group took me aside to discuss the morning's activities. Much to my surprise this is what he said:

"We are really enjoying your seminar, Barry. What I have appreciated more than anything is that you have not used one trendy buzz word during your morning session, and I can't tell you how refreshing that is. We are sick and tired of speakers peppering their lectures with the latest trendy expression. Thank you for that".

Who knew?

To summarize: Words matter. What you say matters. Select your words to fit the tone that you want to set.

PART FIVE

———◆———

7 KEYS TO NEGOTIATING LIKE A PRO

Throughout this book I have shared with you many of my experiences as a parent and business coach. Offering you a series of game plans and strategies to help you gain agreement in every conceivable scenario. Let me conclude by sharing a check list of seven keys to success that professional negotiators live by. These are in no particular order of priority because if you have all seven of them going for you it does not matter what order they are in. This is also not a definitive list, but it does form a good summary of the messages in my book.

CREDIBILITY

Always do what you say you are going to do.

During a speaking career that includes over 2000 presentations worldwide and spans over more than 20 years, in all that time I have missed only one engagement, and that was because bad weather had closed Boston's Logan airport. I mention this only because, regardless of the degree of difficulty in getting to my destination, I never lose sight of my promise to a customer. They expect me to be there on time and ready to go. I never fail to do that, even if I have been paid in full in advance, or perhaps, especially if I have been paid in full in advance.

A promise is a sacred vow, whether given to a business acquaintance or a family member. The rule never changes. If you say you are going to do it, do it. Or don't say it. Never make idle threats or false promises in negotiations. Successful deals require that the other party believes that

177

you will do what you say you are going to do, for better or worse. Build a reputation as someone whose word can be trusted and never under any circumstances allow yourself to be caught in a bluff. Credibility is the foundation upon which all negotiations rest.

PERSONALITY

EMPATHIZE, DON'T CRITICIZE

I made the point earlier in this book that people don't like to do things for people they don't like. Know your personality and make sure it does not inhibit your ability to relate to others. Avoid displaying any annoying little personality habits that may irritate others; such as interrupting the other party mid sentence, or belittling their opinions, or dismissing their argument without even considering it.

In this context, I read an article recently that referred to five things people hate about a sales pitch. As I read the article it occurred to me that they were all personality traits that could be controlled or managed. Here is the list:

Poor vocabulary
Talking too much
Lack of professionalism

Not building rapport
Being ego driven

A good way to analyze the effectiveness of your personality as a means to securing agreement is to think about what you dislike in the personality of others. Consider the personal habits that annoy you when displayed by others and avoid displaying them yourself. Because you can be fairly confident that what annoys you is much the same as that which annoys everyone else.

LOCATION

CONTROL THE TIME AND PLACE

There is no doubt that the party that feels most comfortable with the time and place of any negotiation will have greater control of the outcome. History is plagued by negotiations that were stalled simply because one party or the other felt slighted by the seating arrangements; as depicted in the Paris peace talks which were designed to find a way to end the Vietnam conflict. Or with the Bosnian peace accord that was held at Dayton air force base in Ohio in 1995 which, as legend has it, was selected as the location for the negotiations because it could provide suitable accommodations for all parties, thereby ensuring that none of the attending generals felt slighted.

Selecting the right time and place to resolve issues, whether they be with family members or business acquaintances is an integral part of successful negotiations. I have relayed several examples of this already, including emphasizing the importance of selecting a location that will create a relaxed atmosphere and enhance the process of problem solving.

EXPERTISE

ALWAYS MAKE SURE YOUR FACTS ARE CORRECT AND WELL DOCUMENTED

Nothing will sabotage a negotiation faster than not having your facts straight. Never state that something is a fact unless you can back it up with proof. As the saying goes; "you are entitled to your own opinions but not your own facts". Always be prepared to show supporting evidence for your facts, particularly if the other party is inclined to disbelieve you at face value. Explain your facts in simple to understand language, pausing as necessary to answer any questions of clarification, making sure that each fact is accepted and understood before moving on. The more involved or complex your factual arguments are the more important it becomes to simplify your message. There is an expression that goes; "How do you eat an elephant? Answer: one bite at a time."

Conversely, do not accept what you are told by the other party as a fact without first checking to establish the validity of their position. Just because someone says something is true does not make it a fact. People often present their long held opinions as if they were recognized facts without ever checking to see if what they are saying is true. Always ask for proof whenever the other party posits an argument based on facts. If proof is not readily available then stop negotiating until they can provide the proof. If no proof is forthcoming then discount what they are saying as being a fact and don't allow it to influence your decision making process.

INFORMATION

WHAT YOU KNOW ABOUT THE NEEDS OF THE OTHER PARTY

If I had to single out one of the *7 keys to negotiating like a pro* as being the most important, it would be information. In every aspect of negotiations understanding the needs and agenda of the other party is the card that trumps all others.

Earlier in this book I told the story of a house I purchased from an investment company. I used that example to illustrate the importance of three different strategies:

1. Decision maker.
2. Control the location.
3. Get the agenda.

By using each strategy to my advantage I was able to secure a very satisfying deal. Or at least that is what I believed at the time. Some months later one of the senior employees of that investment company bought the house next door and we became friends as well as neighbors. One time at a back yard barbeque he casually mentioned that the house that I purchased from his company represented a large part of their profit for that year. Now, if I had known that information at the time.....well who knows?

The message from that anecdote is that there is no substitute for information. The more knowledge you have about the needs and desires of the other party the greater control you will have over the outcome of your negotiations. This is equally true whether dealing with your children, friends or business acquaintances, as I have demonstrated consistently throughout this book.

Information is also of great value to you in retail transactions. In this modern internet driven world there is a wealth of information available to all of us that levels the playing field in retail negotiations. Whether buying a car or a house, or just shopping for the best bargains on household goods, you can readily gather information on the internet to ascertain whether the asking price is fair. Simply by doing price comparisons from store to store or company to company you can establish if a price is negotiable without ever having to do any of the leg work that was previously required. FYI, every item for sale is negotiable, you just need information to establish the negotiating range and you need to be dealing with someone who has the authority to negotiate.

This brings me to my next point.

TITLE/AUTHORITY

YOUR PERCEIVED POWER
TO MAKE DECISIONS

As parents my wife and I made a pact that we would never override each others authority in the decision making process with our children. We made it clear to our sons early on that there was no way that they could play one of us against the other. If I said no to something my wife would never reverse that decision and of course, vise versa. For a parent to be taken seriously by a child the parental authority must be absolute with no higher or alternative authority available for the child to manipulate.

Managed properly this singular authority message works well in the parent child relationship, but requires more nuance in business transactions. In fact, in business transactions I would argue that singular authority or managerial titles such as vice president, director or supervisor can present ego problems in negotiations.

Case in point: I stated in an earlier story that I was president of a youth soccer club when my son was a teenager. Part of my job responsibility was to ensure that the club affairs were managed smoothly. This was sometimes a challenge with so many parents wanting their child to have maximum playing time, but all in all it was a rewarding experience. I do recall one occasion; however, when remembering to keep my ego in check was important.

One of our regular season games got cancelled because of weather related issues and the coach of our team was having a hard time rescheduling with the coach of the other team. This became a matter of some priority because the winner of this postponed game would qualify for the state championship play offs and the losing team would not. The coaches could not agree on a rescheduling date, whichever date one liked the other coach did not because of availability of players so late in the season with family vacations being a factor. I mention this because I received a phone call at my home from the coach of the other team. Out of frustration he decided to go over the head of our coach and call the president of the team. When I took the phone call from the apposing team's coach he proceeded to ask me if I was the president of the club. When I replied that I was he said. "Good, because I know as president you can make an instant decision". I resisted the urge to say that I could. This was a time for me to defer authority not succumb to it. I told the coach that I would have to clear it with the board of directors, and my own coach.

The point here is that a managerial title can leave you open to having your ego flattered in a negotiation, causing you to make snap decisions in order to look impressive. When that happens, if you are feeling pressured, defer authority using a partner, your own supervisor, or board of directors to get you off the hook.

By the way, there is no reason for you not to reverse the strategy and use this 'appeal to their authority' technique on the other party when it is to your advantage to flatter their ego. All is fair in love and negotiations.

To summarize: When you want to impose your will make your authority appear absolute, but when you are being pressured defer your authority to another party.

REWARDS/CONSEQUENCES

LET THE OTHER PARTY KNOW THE REWARDS OF THEIR CHOICES

There is a saying in business that goes. "You have to be ruthless to be successful". My take on this is that you don't have to be ruthless to be successful, but you do have to be prepared to be ruthless if necessary. The same principle applies to negotiations. You don't have to make power plays to be a successful negotiator, but you do have to be prepared to make them as needed. I am not impressed with people who use threats constantly to intimidate in the negotiating process as that inevitably leads to confrontation and conflict. Conversely, I have little patience with people who avoid conflict at all costs by telling the other party what they think they want to hear. I mention this only because in my experience some people are afraid of the consequences of confrontation and therefore resist saying or doing anything that may upset or disappoint the other party. Don't let that be you.

Letting people know the rewards or consequences of their behavior is an important aspect of negotiating effectively. Handled well it forces the other party to reflect on the impact of their choices, adding another dimension to their decision making process. I mentioned earlier in this book that *Power* as a persuasive element works best when you first establish the value of your *Logic* and *Emotion*. Those beings so, once you have demonstrated that your position is right and fair, don't be afraid to add an impact statement to seal the deal. If you don't articulate the consequences how can you be sure that they know what they are? Don't leave it to chance, even if the conversation makes you feel uncomfortable, always let the other party know what will happen if you don't get agreement. That way they have the opportunity to change their position without you having to actually impose your sanctions.

So there it is: *The 7 keys to negotiating like a pro.* They should serve as a good summary of all the points I have made in this book.

CREDIBILITY
PERSONALITY
LOCATION
EXPERTISE
INFORMATION

AUTHORITY
REWARD/CONSEQUENCES

Always keep them in mind when preparing for an important negotiation and make sure that you are ready on every level.

As a means to assess your readiness to negotiate a solution to any problem you should rate yourself on a scale of 1 to 10 in each of the seven categories. If you score less than 5 out of 10 in any area you need to rethink your position before you go any further. One more thing, if you think that you score 10 out of 10 in all seven categories you are clearly delusional.

There is no such thing as perfection in life, but strive for it nonetheless because the more problems you can solve through negotiations the better your life will be. As Winston Churchill once said: "Jaw, Jaw is better than war, war".

END

Made in the USA
Lexington, KY
21 October 2015